I0093146

Healing Mushrooms

A Comprehensive Guide to Using Medicinal Mushrooms

By: Barton Press

Copyright © 2021 by Barton Press

ALL RIGHTS RESERVED

No part of this book may be reproduced, stored in a retrieval system, or transmitted in any form or by any means, electronic, mechanical, photocopying, recording, scanning, or otherwise, without the prior written permission of the publisher.

Limit of Liability/Disclaimer of Warranty: the publisher and the author make no representations or warranties with respect to the accuracy or completeness of the contents of this work and specifically disclaim all warranties, including without limitation warranties of fitness for a particular purpose. No warranty may be created or extended by sales or promotional materials. The advice and strategies contained herein may not be suitable for every situation. This work is sold with the understanding that the publisher is not engaged in rendering medical, legal or other professional advice or services. If professional assistance is required, the services of a competent professional person should be sought. Neither the publisher nor the author shall be liable for damages arising herefrom. The fact that an individual, organization or website is referred to in this work as a citation and/or potential source of further information does not mean that the author or the publisher endorses the information the individuals, organization or website may provide or recommendations they/it may make. Further, readers should be aware that websites listed on this work may have changed or disappeared between when this work was written and when it is read.

Table of contents

Mushroom Basics...1

Taxonomy and Other Classifications 3

Ecology of Fungi..6

Identification 12

History of Medicinal Mushroom Use.................................14

    Traditional Chinese Medicine.................................15

    East Meets West: Modern Mushrooms...............17

Benefits of Medicinal Mushrooms 20

    Nutritional Value of Mushrooms..........................21

    Through the Lens of Traditional Chinese Medicine.............22

Examples of the Positive Effects of Medicinal Mushrooms
....28

    Case Study 1...28

    Case Study 2...29

    Case Study 3...30

The Mushrooms 31

Acquiring Medicinal Mushrooms 76

    Foraging..76

    Buying Fresh...77

    Buying Dried or Prepared...................................77

    Growing Your Own..79

    Storing Fresh Mushrooms...................................80

Incorporating Mushrooms Into Your Diet.........................81

    General Tips and Preparation..............................81

    Medicinal Preparations.......................................82

    Dosing 84

Recipes **85**

  Reishi Tea 85

  Chaga Tea 86

  Chaga Anti-Inflammatory Smoothie 87

  Golden Mushroom Milk 88

  Mushroom Butter Coffee 89

  Mushroom Cold Brew Iced Tea............................90

  Medicinal Mushroom Broth 91

  Shiitake Stir Fry 92

  Nabemono..94

  Mushroom Stroganoff...96

  Creamy Mushroom Soup 97

  Porcini Risotto 98

  Lion's Mane Burgers 100

  Alfredo Mushroom Pasta.................................... 101

  Mushroom and Avocado Sushi 103

  Italian Mushroom Omelet................................... 105

  Pepper and Mushroom Fajitas............................ 107

  Stuffed Portobello Mushrooms............................ 110

  Mushroom Curry 111

  Vegetarian "Beef" and Broccoli 114

  Parmesan "Cheese" 116

Common Ailments **118**

  Adaptogens 118

  Alzheimer's... 120

  Antibacterial 120

  Anti-Inflammatory 121

  Antioxidants.. 123

  Cancer and Tumors 124

  Diabetes 128

Fatigue and Physical Performance 129

Gut Health 130

Heart Health 131

Immune System 132

Respiratory Problems... 134

Weight Loss 134

Conclusion **136**

Sources... **137**

Mushroom Basics

Mushrooms have been used and consumed worldwide for thousands of years, both as a food and a medicine. Many people enjoy hunting for mushrooms, with some traveling thousands of miles or spending exorbitant amounts of money to find a medicinal mushroom that helps them. Consuming mushrooms for food is generally a healthy habit, as they have a small amount of unsaturated fats, while providing necessary nutrients such as protein and carbohydrates. Most cultures in the Western world have not come to appreciate and understand mushrooms in the same way that people in many other parts of the world do. Americans usually only have access to *Agaricus bisporus*, also known as the button mushroom. This species, often found in fields and meadows, is nutritionally mediocre and bland in flavor, which would understandably lead to a cultural distaste for mushrooms.

There are over 100,000 species of fungi, of which around 38,000 can be considered mushrooms. Most of these mushroom species flourish on the floor of forests around the world, living on the decay and waste of the rest of the forest. While most plants take in carbon dioxide and release oxygen, mushrooms actually consume oxygen and then release carbon dioxide, similar to the breath of humans. Their off gassed carbon dioxide can then be reused by plants, continuing the circle of life. While mushrooms and fungi may seem like plants to uninformed people, they are actually a very different organism with their own methods of growth and reproduction. The umbrella shaped fruiting body, commonly referred to as a "mushroom", is only one part of a fungus' growth and life cycle.

When fungi break down matter for consumption, they release enzymes into the substance that breaks down large compounds into smaller compounds. Not only are the fungi then able to consume it, but the decomposing matter also enriches the soil and allows plants and trees to consume the nutrients. Fungi play an important symbiotic role with many plants and animals, and some fungal species even have an exclusive relationship with a specific plant.

Throughout history, ancient peoples have experimented with and appreciated the positive effects of medicinal mushrooms. Anthropological evidence tells that humans have been using mushrooms as medicine for at least 5000 years. The history of medicinal mushrooms is especially rich in traditional Chinese medicine. In 1578, a traditional Chinese medicine practitioner collected his knowledge into a book that featured detailed descriptions and uses for 20 medicinal mushrooms. Recently, Chinese books and publications have been produced that detail over 800 medicinal mushrooms and their uses.

Traditional Chinese medicine usually takes a holistic approach to curing illnesses and ailments. Ideally, proper health starts with a healthy lifestyle and preventive care, rather than only treating conditions as they come along. Preventive care can include daily exercise, a well-balanced diet, and a healthy living environment free of pollution, excessive noise, and other external stresses. If you submit yourself to a lethargic lifestyle and eat poorly, you can expect to experience weight gain, heart disease, diabetes, cancer, and other health conditions. After you have addressed the root of a health condition, then medicinal mushrooms can be used to help guide your body back to health.

Today, modern science has been taking a dive into medicinal mushrooms and their benefits. Many studies have been conducted focusing on the potential of medicinal mushrooms to aid in a variety of diseases and ailments, including cancer, diabetes, respiratory illness, weight loss, and more. In many cases, these studies only confirm what traditional folk medicine has known all along.

Taxonomy and Other Classifications

Most people are familiar with the basics of taxonomy from their high school biology classes. Every living thing on Earth can be classified according to a set of widely accepted naming rules. There are a few different "kingdoms" to which a species can belong to. For example, humans are part of the "Animalia" kingdom, plants belong to the "Plantae" kingdom, and mushrooms and fungi make up the "Fungi" kingdom.

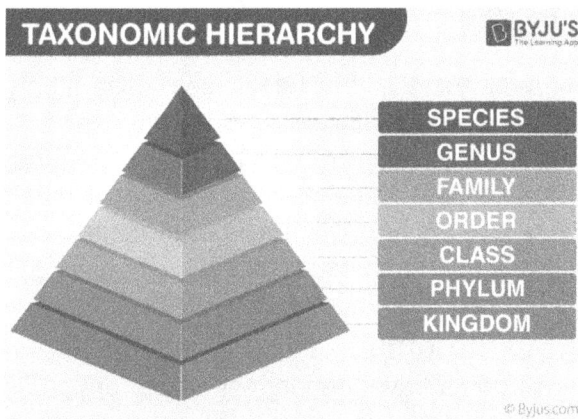

For a fungus to be recognized by scientists and mycologists (those who study the fungi kingdom), the species must be given a taxonomic name. The name must adhere to internationally accepted rules. Like all other organisms, such as *Homo sapien*, the name is a binomial and consists of the genus and the species.

For example, the species *Amanita muscaria* is a widely known and identifiable mushroom. It is the classic red mushroom with white spots, commonly featured in children's books and video games. This species belongs to the genus *Amanita (note the A. in the names below*, which includes over 600 individual species including *A. zambiana*, *A. basii*, and *A. muscaria*. Most of the mushrooms belonging to the class *Amanita* are toxic or poisonous, including *A. muscaria*. However, toxicity is not what leads to a species being classified as *Amanita*. The genus is related by their white spore prints, mostly dry caps, warts or patches on the caps, and other visual identifications.

You may also see species names listed with a scientist's name who first studied, identified, or reclassified the species. For instance, *Ganoderma lucidum* is sometimes referred to as *G. lucidum* (W. Curt.: Fr.) P. Karsten. This means that mycologist W. Curt initially discovered and classified the species, while P. Karsten made additional contributions to the classification and study of the species. For the sake of simplicity, we will try to avoid this naming system in this book and stick with the basic *"Genus species"* naming conventions.

Common names for the fruiting bodies (also known as the sporophore) of a fungus include "mushroom" and "toadstool". Edible varieties are often referred to as mushrooms, while poisonous and unsafe varieties are usually called toadstools. These names have no scientific basis and either can be used to refer to the fleshy sporophores of a fungus.

Polypore Mushrooms
Polypore mushrooms have the longest history of use as medicine in ancient cultures. Polypores are the tough, woody mushrooms usually found on trees. They are characterized by large fruiting bodies and tubes or pores for spore dispersal on their underside. Polypores are often referred to as "bracket" or "shelf" fungi and their fruiting bodies are called "conks". Notable polypore species include *Ganoderma lucidum* (reishi), *Trametes versicolor* (turkey tail), and *Inonotus obliquus* (chaga).

Saprobe/Saprobic/Saprotrophic
Saprobic fungi consume decomposing or decaying organic material. They are the only multicellular organisms with the ability to process and digest cellulose and lignin, two varieties of cellular

proteins. Not all wood-rotting species are saprobic, as some fungi are parasitic and grow in living wood.

Parasitic

Parasitic fungi attack living organisms to obtain their nourishment. They make their homes in plants, trees, insects, and even other mushrooms. In many cases, parasitic fungi will eventually kill their hosts (such as a dying tree), wherein the fungi would then be classified as saprobic.

Mycorrhizal

Mycorrhizal fungi become involved in a mutually beneficial relationship with a host plant. This relationship is called a "mycorrhiza". Usually, this relationship involves the mycelium of a fungus playing an important role in the plant's "rhizosphere", which is another term for "root system" or "root area".

Mycorrhizal relationships are further classified into two categories: ectomycorrhizas and endomycorrhizas. The mycelium of ectomycorrhizal fungi do not penetrate the individual cells of a plant's roots, while endomycorrhizal fungi do penetrate the cell walls.

Ectomycorrhizal fungi often create a "hartig net". In this case, the mycelium of a fungus creates a sheath around the plant's roots and can then transfer nutrients to the plant from anywhere in the mycelium network. Some of these fungi have been known to transfer nutrients between different plants, including trees of different species.

A mycorrhizal species would usually be in contrast to a parasitic fungus, which attacks its host plant. However, there are some cases of parasitic mycorrhizal fungi.

Ecology of Fungi

Fungi have a heavy burden on their shoulders: they are responsible for decomposing and recycling nature's waste. This role, similar to that of bacteria, is important to the balance of most ecosystems. Fungi break down organic waste that would otherwise be left unprocessed and not recycled. Many plants also rely on certain species of fungi to create symbiotic, or "mycorrhizal", relationships. These mycorrhizal fungi have created a relationship with a specific plant in which they rely on each other for nutrients and survival.

Fungi and their popular "fruits", mushrooms, can be found worldwide. They reside in obvious places such as forests and grassy fields, but also in harsh environments like the desert or the arctic. Because of their prolific and unique method of reproduction (most species of mushroom can send out millions of spores in one day), they can spread fast and have reached most corners of the globe.

Not only are fungi found in nature, but they also play a big role in everyday human life. Beer, cheese, bread, and other fermented products would not be possible without fungi. Not only are they used to process foods, but fungi can produce edible mushrooms fit for human consumption. Many compounds found in edible mushrooms provide potent medicinal benefits, as well as quality nutrition.

Nature's Recyclers

The circle of life would be incomplete without organisms that can decompose and recycle organic material. Fungi consume matter in a "backwards" fashion when compared to most other organisms. They begin by digesting their food before ingesting it by releasing enzymes that break large molecules into smaller ones. This process also releases nutrients, such as nitrogen and phosphorus, into the environment for other plants to use and consume.

Fungi and Humans

Fungi may seem like a nuisance to many people. If you have ever dealt with moldy fruit or had experience with a fungal infection, you might be repulsed at the idea of fungi. However, there are many positive benefits and species of fungi that heavily outweigh the few "bad apples".

Many fungi species have adapted to attack certain insects. The agriculture industry has been exploring these species as possible natural alternatives to chemical insecticides. The fungus *Beauveria bassiana* is commercially available and is used to control a variety of pests including whitefly, aphids, borers, weevils, and others. Natural remedies such as this are a great step forward in an agricultural industry plagued with harmful chemical pesticides.

Mycorrhizal relationships also play a large role in the agriculture industry. Farm-land requires these fungi to partner with plant's root systems to maximize production. In fact, over 75% of trees and grasses require mycorrhizal fungi to survive. Commercial soil amendments containing fungal cultures are available allowing farmers to add beneficial fungi to their soil.

In many parts of the world, mushrooms make up a significant portion of human diets. Shiitakes, chanterelles, morels, and oysters are popular examples of edible mushrooms. Most mushrooms have a meaty texture, earthy flavor, and plenty of nutrients. As you may know, many species of fungi are known to provide potent medicinal benefits. Before the pharmaceutical age that we are currently in, mushrooms were a respected and often used medicine for a variety of ailments. In recent decades, modern science has caught on to the use of mushrooms, as studies and experiments have been proving again, what traditional medicine has known all along: mushrooms can heal!

Humans learned how to control fermentation thousands of years ago, right around the time that "civilization" started to take over the hunter-gatherer lifestyle. Residue found on pottery jars of an ancient village in China revealed that humans were fermenting beverages as early as 7000 BCE! The early alcoholic beverage was crafted from rice, honey, and fruit. Fermentation of food and beverage like this would not be possible without fungi. Yeast (a type of fungi) processes sugar into carbon dioxide and ethyl alcohol when kept in anaerobic conditions. This chemical process makes things like beer, wine, and spirits possible. Species of *Penicillium* are responsible for the production of blue, soft cheeses, while *Scopulariopsis* is used to create harder cheeses. Another staple of the human diet, bread, is only made possible by fungi. When yeast is introduced to bread dough, the fungus eats away the sugars in the dough and produces carbon dioxide, which gives bread dough its fluffy, airy texture.

Recently, inconsiderate forestry practices have led to a decline in species diversity and the threatening and possible extinction of some mushroom species. As more and more forests are cleared, the available habitat for fungi continues to shrink. Even if these areas are replanted, mycorrhizal species suffer (those that have a mutually beneficial relationship with a specific plant). Clearing a forest can actually cause a short burst of overall fungi activity in an area (due to the increased availability of dead wood and other decaying material), but at the cost of eliminating mycorrhizal species that relied on specific trees or plants in the area. In these cases, the increase in fungi activity is short lived, unnatural, and unsustainable.

Mushroom Biology

While there are different life cycles and different methods of reproduction throughout the fungi world, we will focus on the classic spore, mycelium, and mushroom dynamic found in most medicinal mushrooms.

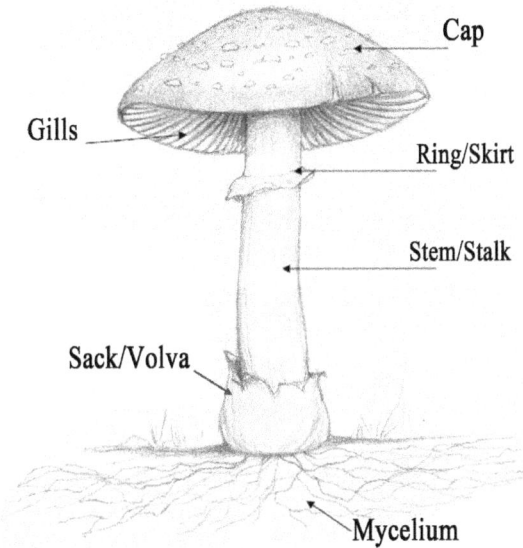

Cap

Gills

Ring/Skirt

Stem/Stalk

Sack/Volva

Mycelium

Spores

Most fungi start life as a "spore", which are similar in idea to the seeds of plants and are sometimes called "fungal seeds". Spores are produced and released by the fruiting bodies of fungi through their gills or pores. One mushroom can output inconceivable amounts of spores, but most of these do not find adequate growing conditions. When fungal spores find appropriate moisture, temperature, and nutrient conditions, they will germinate and start producing an underground network of strands called mycelium. This first stage of a fungus' life cycle is similar to the idea of a plant's seed germinating and producing roots.

Fungal spores are everywhere - in the air, on surfaces, and in every breath you take. Luckily, they are harmless, at least in the case of most mushroom spores. Other fungi, such as mold and mildew, are a different story.

Mycelium

Once a spore has properly germinated, mycelium growth occurs. The mycelium is the vegetative part of a fungus composed of a network of thin filaments, similar in idea to the roots of a plant. It takes in the necessary nutrients to grow and produce fruiting bodies. A new mycelium begins when spores from mushrooms find their way into favorable conditions and germinate into hyphae. Hyphae are thin, feathery filaments that grow to produce the white web of mycelium. These mycelium can grow to epic proportions when given the chance. In fact, one mycelium specimen of the honey mushroom (*Armillaria solidipes*) holds the record for the largest known organism on Earth. The mycelium covers almost 4 square miles of the Malheur National Forest in Oregon. It is over 2,000 years old and might weigh as much as 35,000 tons!

The mycelium of a fungus usually has the biggest ecological impact on an area, as opposed to the fruiting bodies or spores. In mycorrhizal relationships with other plants, the mycelium often acts as a net. It creates a sheath around the root systems of plants and trees, transferring water and nutrients to and from plants as needed. Mycelium are also responsible for releasing the enzymes that decay and decompose dead (and sometimes living) organic matter. The mycelium absorbs the nutrients to form a fruiting body, and the plant is decomposed into healthy soil ready to welcome the growth of new flora.

If that isn't enough, mycelium can actually help plants communicate with each other. Mycelium can transfer information about water and nutrient location and transfer nutrients from one plant to another, and even between plants of different species. The plants pay the mushrooms for their service in the form of carbohydrates.

Fruiting Bodies

The fruiting bodies of fungi, also called mushrooms, conks, sporophores, and a variety of other names, are the visible part of a fungus. To avoid confusion, we will usually use the term "mushroom" to refer to any fruiting body of a fungus. The term "conk" will be used to describe the tough and woody fruiting bodies of polypore species, such as *Ganoderma lucidum* and *Fomes fomentarius*. The mushrooms that you see on a tree are an example of a sporophore. Mushrooms come in a wide range of colors, shapes, and sizes. Some are as small as a grain of rice, while others can grow to immense sizes. Many of the fruiting bodies of our medicinal fungi species are a classic "mushroom" shape with a cap (pileus) and usually a stem (stape). Gills are found underneath the cap on most mushrooms. Some mushrooms have a ring around the stem that is often attached to the cap. Other mushrooms may have a cup (volva) around the base of the stem.

Mushrooms grow to continue the life cycle of a fungus. When environmental conditions are favorable, the mycelium will send up mushrooms to release spores and start the process all over again. One mushroom can send out millions or billions of spores, but usually only a few of these spores are able to find a favorable environment and germinate into a new mycelium.

Most mushrooms are annuals, producing fruiting bodies at one time every year. Some polypore species are perennial and usually grow a new layer every year. While the mycelium plays an important part in nature, the fruiting bodies of fungi have played the biggest role in providing food and medicine for humans for centuries.

Identification

Mushroom identification is a skill that takes knowledge and skill to accurately perform. Some mushrooms require a true master to properly identify. Mushroom poisoning is a common occurrence that should not be taken lightly. Poisoning usually occurs when a look-alike is misidentified as an edible mushroom. Never consume a mushroom unless you are absolutely positive of its identity!

The best way to learn mushroom identification is through a class or mushroom club. Your local botanical garden or university may offer classes. Otherwise, going on a mushroom hunt with somebody knowledgeable in the field is the best way to gain experience. While a field guide-book can be a fun way to identify species, if you are thinking about using wild mushrooms for food or medicine, there is no substitute for a local and knowledgeable instructor or guide.

Most mushrooms can be identified through a few key metrics, including the appearance, the habitat, and the spore print. Only through practice and study will you be able to confidently identify mushrooms in the wild.

Appearance

Judging and recognizing the appearance of a mushroom is the first step to identification. The shape, color, and structure of a mushroom all need to be considered when attempting to identify a mushroom. The appearance can change as a mushroom grows, so you may need to collect immature and mature specimens to properly identify a species.

Habitat

The habitat in which a fungus is growing is a big factor in identification. There are many look-alike species that are only distinguishable by *where* they grow, as opposed to the color or shape of the mushrooms. The habitat could be a grassy lawn, a meadow, or a forest.

For further certainty in identification, the substrate on which the mushroom is growing must be identified as well. The substrate is the material from which the mushrooms emerge. The substrate may say a lot about a mushroom species, as many fungi are picky about where they call "home" and may only develop in one specific substrate. Examples of possible substrates include a dead oak tree, at the base of a living pine tree, or even the body of insect larvae (as in the case of *Cordyceps* species).

Spore Prints

If further identification is needed, then a spore print can be created and analyzed. The color and structure of a mushroom's spore deposit will help differentiate it from other look-alike species.

To take a spore print, start by cutting off the cap from a fresh mushroom. Next, place the cap on a white piece of paper with the gills facing down. Place the cap in a safe space with a cup or other protective item over the top to prevent it from moving. After about eight hours, you may remove the cap. You should see an inky print on the piece of paper: this is the spore print. If there is no spore print visible, the spores may be white or light colored, so you will need to use a dark piece of paper. If you still can't see a print, you may have collected an immature or sterile specimen.

History of Medicinal Mushroom Use

Mushrooms and fungi have been used as a natural medicine for thousands of years. Prior to our current world's obsession with pharmaceutical drugs, mushrooms were a widely used natural medicine. A poem found on the walls of ancient Egyptian temples has been translated as follows:

"Without leaves, without buds, without flowers:
Yet they form fruit.
As a food, as a tonic, as a medicine;
The entire creation is precious."

The Egyptians were just one of many cultures that used and appreciated mushrooms. Ötzi was an ancient man that was frozen in a glacier for around 5000 years, until his discovery in 1991. He was found in the Ötzal Alps, near Italy and Austria. Among his belongings were two mushroom species, one of which was the birch fungus, a medicinal mushroom known to have antiparasitic properties. Ötzi was one of the world's first "mycologists"!

In MesoAmerica, the use of hallucinogenic mushrooms and cacti dates back around 5000 years according to archaeological evidence. The substances were used in rituals and ceremonies to achieve intoxication and induce states of trance. We also have more than archaeological evidence for the use of mushrooms in MesoAmerican culture, as the local shamans in the area still use these practices in ceremonies today.

Hippocrates, the Greek physician, was one of the first people to document and classify a mushroom. Around 450 BCE, he acknowledged the anti-inflammatory and wound-healing properties of *Fomes fomentarius*. Similarly, Chinese medicine provided written records for many different mushrooms beginning around 100 BCE. In fact, some of the richest history and deepest knowledge can be found in the writings and history of traditional Chinese medicine.

Traditional Chinese Medicine

Traditional Chinese medicine has some of the richest history of medicinal mushroom use. In 1578, Li Shizhen wrote a landmark book, *Bencao Gangmu*, covering many aspects of Chinese medicine. The book, also called *Compendium of Materia Medica*, was a product of Shizhen's travels and medical practice in the field, as well as rigorous study of over 800 medical books. *Compendium* features descriptions and references for over 1,800 medicinal substances, including 20 species of medicinal mushroom. Most of traditional Chinese medicine, even in modern times, is based on *Compendium*, as well as another text, *Huangdi Neijing*.

Huangdi Neijing, also known as the *Yellow Emperor's Inner Classic*, is arguably the most important Chinese medicine text, as well as being a major book in the Daoist philosophical tradition. The book is thought to have been recorded sometime between 475 BCE and 220 CE. The text is modeled as a conversation between the Yellow Emperor and his physicians or scribes. The Yellow Emperor, or Huangdi, was a god in Chinese folk religions and was the first emperor and leader of China. Some scholars believe that the book was written in this anonymous way to avoid persecution, as the ideas in the book were new and possibly scandalous at the time.

Huangdi Neijing was revolutionary because it abandoned old beliefs that death and disease were caused by demons and spirits. Instead, it was asserted that natural causes are the reason for disease, such as diet, environment, lifestyle, and emotions. According to the book, the universe is governed and constructed of different forces and principles, such as yin and yang, qi, and wuxing. Through proper care of one's diet, emotions, and other natural phenomena, one can balance and live in harmony with these forces, potentially keeping you free from disease. This is a basic interpretation of these principles, and interested parties should explore the history and guidelines of traditional Chinese medicine in further detail.

Zhang Zhongjing, often known as the "Chinese Hippocrates", was a Chinese physician who is famous for his 3rd century CE writings, entitled *Shang han za bing lun* (*Treatise on Febrile and Other Diseases*). The writings were later edited and split into two books, *Treatise on Febrile Diseases* and *Jingui Collection of Prescriptions*. Zhang's works were important additions to the field of dietetics, as well as providing quality information about typhoid and other fevers.

Over the following centuries, traditional Chinese medicine continued to develop and become more refined. Other immortalized medical practitioners, such as Hua Tuo and Wang Shuhe, continued to experiment and make improvements on the knowledge of their ancestors. It was not until the 16th century that Western medicine began to show up in China. Around that time, a Portuguese Bishop established Saint Raphael's Hospital in China. As Western medicine spread through the country, some Chinese people began to favor and trust Western medicine over traditional forms, probably due to it being more "scientific" or the like. This faith in Western medicine continued to spread, but interest in traditional Chinese medicine was restored in the early 20th century.

This renewal of interest in traditional medicines coincides with a great migration of Chinese people to the U.S. in the 19th and 20th centuries, who labored on railroads and in mines. These immigrants brought traditional Chinese medicine with them, although these methods were not accepted and used outside of Chinese communities until late in the 20th century.

In 1971, a New York Times reporter, James Reston, traveled to China and had to be treated for appendicitis while in the country. He received emergency surgery for the appendicitis, followed by a round of acupuncture to alleviate some pain in his intestine and stomach. The acupuncture was a success and inspired Reston to write about his experiences with Chinese medicine in a New York Times article, *Now About My Operation in Peking*. This article has often been credited as one of the first introductions of traditional Chinese medicine to the general American public.

In 1980, two Chinese professors compiled their book, *Fungi Pharmacopoeia*, regarding medicinal mushrooms and their traditional uses. The book covers over 120 medicinal mushroom species and goes into details about the diseases and conditions each mushroom can be used for. In 1987, another book was written by five Chinese scientists, entitled *Icons of Medicinal Fungi from China*. The book gives details and descriptions of over 272 medicinal mushroom species, over twice as many as *Fungi Pharmacopoeia*. In 2013, yet another compendium of information was published, entitled *Medicinal Fungi of China*. The book was written by Wu Xinglian, Mao Xiolan, and others and covers over 800 medicinal mushroom species with sources from around 2400 scientific articles.

Today, mushrooms like turkey tails are used in conjunction with modern medicine to help fight cancer in some East Asian countries. Shiitake mushrooms have been consumed in China, Japan, and other Asian countries for thousands of years, both for their nutritional and medicinal benefits.

East Meets West: Modern Mushrooms

Modern science has yet to fully explore and embrace the benefits of medicinal mushrooms. In his book *Supernatural Horror in Literature*, H.P. Lovecraft wrote that "the oldest and strongest kind of fear is fear of the unknown." Eating a mushroom might nourish you, poison you, or send you on a spiritual journey. This uncertainty has certainly inspired a fear of mushrooms in the general population, especially in the Western world where medicinal mushrooms are not ingrained in the culture and history.

Another factor for the lack of research into medicinal mushrooms is the rarity and quick life-cycle of a mushroom. While mycelium can live hidden underground for hundreds of years, most mushrooms grow and die within a few days and might take a year or more to reappear again. In addition, many species of mushroom are more difficult than plants to domesticate and cultivate. This sort of elusiveness has made it difficult to experiment with and study fungi.

That being said, modern science has finally taken an interest in medicinal mushrooms in the past few decades. Much research and study has gone into isolating the beneficial compounds in mushrooms, mostly with tests on lab animals. Human clinical trials have also begun that build off and confirm the breadth of knowledge and experience provided by ancient traditional medicine. Most research does not delve into confirming or denying traditional uses for the various mushrooms. Rather, most studies seem to attempt to isolate beneficial compounds in the fungi to later be produced into pharmaceuticals. The pharmaceutical industry has a well-documented history of price gouging, creating an opioid addiction problem in America, and other unscrupulous practices. The idea of natural, traditional, time-tested medicines being used in Western medicine seems promising, but the pharmaceutical industry could also abuse their power by patenting and charging exorbitant prices for mushroom-derived products. Only time will tell.

A focus on fresh and healthy foods has caused American mushroom consumption to rise in recent decades. According to the USDA, mushroom consumption in the 1960s averaged at around 1 pound, per person, per year. By the early 2000s, the average American was consuming almost 4 pounds of mushrooms per year. It is also interesting to note the recent switch of preference from dried to fresh mushrooms. In 1994, the average American was consuming 1.93 pounds of dried mushroom products (adjusted for fresh weight equivalency) and 2.02 pounds of fresh mushrooms.

By 2001, dried mushroom consumption had decreased by 30% to 1.35 pounds, while fresh mushroom consumption enjoyed a 28% increase to 2.59 pounds.

Benefits of Medicinal Mushrooms

The simplest benefit that mushrooms can provide is as an excellent source of nutrition. Many mushrooms are considered to be both medicinal and edible. Romans of classical times thought of mushrooms as a "Food of the Gods" and served them at holidays and festivities. Ancient Greek warriors consumed mushrooms as a source of strength for battle, while Egyptian Pharaohs held mushrooms in high esteem as a luxurious food. Today, we know that mushrooms are high in protein, carbohydrates, and fiber, while being low in fat content. They are also a great source of amino acids, vitamins, and minerals, including potassium, phosphorus, thiamine, riboflavin, and niacin. Common edible species, such as shiitake, oyster, and button mushrooms, are safe to consume everyday as a vegetable.

Many medicinal mushrooms are described as containing "adaptogens" or "adaptogenic properties". Adaptogens were first defined by Russian doctors I.I. Brekhman and N.V. Lazarev. They describe adaptogens as "biological response modifiers" that must fit three criteria. First, the substance should cause no harm and place no additional stress on the body. Second, it should help the body to adapt to a variety of environmental and psychological stresses. Finally, it should aid and support a wide variety of functions in the body, such as the immune system, the nervous system, the hormonal system, and regulating functions. Adaptogens can also have an indirect effect on the immune system, creating a defense for the body against a variety of stresses, such as noise, environment, overwork, emotional issues, and more.

If adaptogens can perform even a small amount of these functions, the need for them should be clear. The industrial and technological revolutions have created a whole slew of challenges and stresses for the human body to adapt to, but we have not given our bodies enough time to evolve natural defense mechanisms. Modern science has spent inconceivable amounts of time and money in the fight against cancer, but they have yet to make any real progress towards a cure. Rather, the American Cancer Association often suggests preventative measures, such as changing one's diet and exercising regularly. Consuming mushrooms with adaptogenic properties has been a form of preventative care in traditional Chinese medicine for thousands of years. Considering the high rates of cancer and other issues in modern society, medicinal mushrooms definitely deserve more consideration from the general public.

The effects of medicinal mushrooms on cancer, tumors, and related issues is evident by years of traditional use and many recent medical studies and trials. Polysaccharides and beta-glucans, compounds found in many different medicinal mushrooms, are known to exhibit cytotoxic (tumor cell killing) and immune boosting properties, rallying the bodies defenses and sending aid where it is needed. Cancer prevention has also been explored and suggested, mostly due to the antioxidant effects of compounds found in medicinal mushrooms.

Nutritional Value of Mushrooms

Of the over 100,000 species of fungi, around 2,000 have been confirmed as edible. The number is probably far more, as many species have yet to be discovered or tested for edibility. Fungi are an interesting food source, as they have the ability to transform substances with poor nutrients into a fat and protein rich food source. Edible fungi can be grown on the discarded food scraps and other waste of the world.

While many mushrooms boast medicinal and highly nutritious properties, even the least nutritious mushrooms rank on par with common vegetables. Nutrient quantities can vary between fresh and dried, wild or cultivated, and so on. However, we will try to cover some general information about mushroom nutrition.

Concentrations of protein range between 1-4% of dried weight. *Marasmius oreades*, also known as the fairy ring mushroom, can have a protein content around 5%, while the well-known chanterelle mushroom may only contain around 1.5%. Carbohydrate levels can range between 3% and 28%, depending on the species. Fat content usually ranges between 0.2-0.8% of fresh mushrooms, with essential fatty acids such as linoleic acid being particularly abundant. The stems are particularly rich in these important fatty acids.

Mushrooms tend to be an adequate source of many vitamins, including Vitamin C, riboflavin, niacin, and thiamine. Minerals such as phosphorus, sodium, and potassium are found in relatively high quantities in many mushrooms. It is interesting to note that some species' nutritional value will change with their environment. For instance, some fungi have been known to accumulate heavy metals, such as lead and cadmium, when grown in an area where they are present.

The method of cooking will also have an effect on the nutrient content of mushrooms. The levels of some substances, such as Vitamin C, thiamine, and B vitamins, are known to shrink or disappear completely when heated. Fiber and protein are affected by heat and cooking, but should still be mostly available to your body. Most minerals are not affected by cooking. Lightly stir-frying or sauteing will have a less detrimental effect on the nutrients than boiling the mushrooms in water. It is not advisable to consume mushrooms raw, as some species have negative effects when not cooked through. Check on your specific species of mushrooms for the best methods of cooking.

Through the Lens of Traditional Chinese Medicine

Traditional Chinese medicine practitioners encountered many of the same ailments and illnesses that we experience today. However, they approached the problems in different ways and defined certain illnesses in a different way. TCM practitioners discovered and explained many of the medicinal mushrooms that we know today, so I will try to explain the basic tenets of TCM to provide more context. If the history and alternative views interest you, consider diving into other resources written by TCM practitioners.

TCM describes the body as a multi-faceted system made up of *qi* and *yin-yang* properties known as "functional entities". These functional entities contribute to the body's five "cardinal functions", which are actuation, warming, defense, containment, and transportation. These cardinal functions maintain health and wellness in the body.

Five Fundamental Substances

The first of the functional entities is the Five Fundamental Substances: *Qi, Shen* (Spirit), *Jing* (Essence), *Jinye* (Body Fluids), and *Xue* (Blood).

Qi is the hardest to define, but it is the most discussed and can be thought of as the life force that flows through our bodies. Ancient Chinese people thought of *qi* as the most important entity that makes up our world. The Chinese symbol for qi is actually the same as "air" or "gas" and it is believed to exhibit the same properties as those materials.

Human *qi* is thought to originate from two main sources. The first is the *qi* that we inherit from our parents at conception, also referred to as the "innate vital substance". The second source of qi comes in natural forms, such as the food, water, and air that we consume. Following this idea, we can assume that breathing fresh air and consuming nutritious food like medicinal mushrooms can have a positive effect on our *qi*.

Zang-Fu

The second functional entity is *Zang-Fu*, which refers to an assortment of organs that regulate and promote *qi* in the body. These "organs" should not be thought of in the literal sense that you would find in Western Medicine. Rather, it is a way to explain the interconnectedness and associated functions that produce and control the *qi* in the body.

The "*Zang*" organs are associated with *yin* (darkness or cold). The purpose of the *Zang* organs is to produce and store the Five Fundamental Substances: qi, spirit, essence, body fluids, and blood. The five *Zang* organs are the heart, spleen, lung, kidney, and liver. Each organ has a function, as well as a corresponding physical and emotional element.

The heart is responsible for storing the spirit and is associated with the emotion of joy. Too much joy, or over-excitement, may have a negative impact on the heart. Physically, the heart is associated with blood, blood vessels, pulse, and the "meridians". Symptoms from an imbalance in the heart may include lack of sleep, nightmares, or palpitations.

The spleen is known as a dynamic organ, being responsible for the transportation (a cardinal function) of *qi* and blood from food and water. In addition, the spleen actuates (another cardinal function) the *qi* and blood to the other *Zang* organs. It is associated with emotions like worry, pondering, and dwelling. Physically, the spleen is associated with the limbs. A spleen imbalance can manifest itself in a variety of ways, including excessive fatigue, long or heavy periods, and poor digestion.

The lung is responsible for the transportation and actuation of oxygen and breath through the body. The lung is connected to the emotion of grief, as well as the physical attributes of skin and hair. Symptoms of a lung imbalance include asthma, shortness of breath, fatigue, dry skin, and other issues.

The kidney is known to store *qi* and pass it along to any other organ when in need. Emotionally, it is associated with fear, which can weaken the kidneys and lower *qi*. Physically, it is involved with water intake, retention, and expulsion, as well being connected with the ears and teeth. An imbalance in the kidney can cause a variety of symptoms, including hearing loss, frequent urination, infertility, and other issues.

The liver is associated with the digestion and processing of nutrients, as well as ensuring a smooth flow of *qi* throughout the body. It also stores blood and plays a role in regulating healthy, pain-free periods. Emotionally, the liver is associated with anger. An imbalance in the liver can manifest itself in a variety of ways, including depression, redness in the face, verbal outbursts, and other conditions.

The *fu* organs are associated with *yang* (brightness or warmth). The six *fu* organs are the stomach, small intestine, large intestine, urinary bladder, gallbladder, and *sanjiao*, which lacks an English anatomical translation.

In TCM, the stomach holds extra importance. Food and water first pass through the stomach for digestion. Nutritional *qi* is extracted from the food in the stomach. The "pure" parts of food are sent to the spleen for further transformation, while the "impure" parts are sent to the small intestine.

The small intestine continues to process the material from the stomach. It performs similar actions, separating "pure" and "impure" materials and sending them to their appropriate places. The pure parts are again sent to the spleen, while the impure is sent to the large intestine. Excess water is sent to the bladder to be stored as urine. An imbalance in the small intestine may lead to painful urination or loose stools.

The large intestine receives impure parts of the digested food and is the last step in the processing of food. After this last step of processing and nutrient extraction, the waste products are excreted. An imbalance in the large intestine can lead to abdominal pain and diarrhea.

The gallbladder is closely associated with the liver. It stores and secretes bile that is produced by the liver, similar to ideas found in Western medicine. If the liver has an imbalance, it will affect the gallbladder (and vice versa). An imbalance in the gallbladder can lead to a yellow in the skin and eyes as bile builds up in the body.

The urinary bladder stores and excretes the waste fluids sent by the other *fu* organs. The urinary bladder is closely associated with the lungs, spleen, and kidneys, as they also deal with water and its distribution in the body. An imbalance in the bladder can lead to urination problems and may cause problems with the kidneys or other organs.

Sanjiao is the most difficult to describe and is often translated as "the triple burner". The "triple burner" can be thought of as three sections of the torso: the upper, middle, and lower portions. The three burners are explained in the classic text *Huangdi Neijing*: "The upper burner acts like a mist. The middle burner acts like foam. The lower burner acts like a swamp." "Mist" refers to the *qi*, blood, and bodily fluids that are distributed through the body. "Foam" refers to the digestive processes of the middle part of the body. "Swamp" refers to the expulsion of waste and impure substances.

Jing-Luo
The third functional entity is *Jinq-Luo*. *Qi* is known to flow and permeate through every part of the body. However, it is said to accumulate and move through pathways called "*jing-luo*", or more commonly known as the "meridians". A good representation for the way *qi* travels is to imagine water flowing through nature, always taking the path of least resistance. Similarly, *qi* can pool up in the crevices and divisions inside the body. These areas of collected *qi* are more concentrated and accessible, which makes them open for therapy and manipulation through massage, acupuncture, and other methods.

Medicinal Mushrooms and the Functional Entities

This was just scratching the surface of the knowledge and ideas present in traditional Chinese medicine. Hopefully it helps illustrate the way that proper nutrition and medicinal mushrooms can have positive effects that ripple throughout the body. The "holistic" aspects of TCM are important to understand, as all of the organs and parts of the body are interconnected. When one organ has an imbalance, it can have negative effects on other parts of the body. These ideas also make it easier to trace a problem back to its origin. Western medicine often forgets this holistic approach, only treating a symptom without addressing the cause of that symptom.

Examples of the Positive Effects of Medicinal Mushrooms

Humans have been performing research into the effects of various mushrooms for thousands of years. In ancient times, every time someone decided to eat a new fungus or plant that they discovered, they were performing research and studies (and those studies were dangerous as well - we should be thankful for those who tested out the many inedible mushrooms that are out there). While the "research" was not always well-documented, the traditions and medicines that humans discovered were passed down orally until they began to be recorded a few thousand years ago.

Many recent studies have been performed that further prove and confirm what traditional medicine has told us all along: medicinal mushrooms can play an important role in the health and well-being of people. Below, we have summarized a few of these studies that highlight the effectiveness of medicinal mushrooms on a variety of ailments.

Case Study 1

In a 2010 publication entitled _Medicinal mushroom Phellinus linteus as an alternative cancer therapy_, author Daniel Silva explored the anti-tumor and immune boosting functions of _Phellinus linteus_. In the report, polysaccharide compounds isolated from samples of the fungus _P. linteus_ were found to increase the activity of immune cells in the body. The compounds also increased the cytotoxic activity of the natural killer cells in one's body, such as white blood cells. In the publication, Silva covered three independent case reports that all suggest that _P. linteus_ has a profound effect on reducing the size of cancerous tumors.

The publication covered an experiment with mice that were implanted with melanoma cells. The mice that were treated with _P._

linteus survived significantly longer than control groups. One important note was that the compounds in *P. linteus* did not directly kill the cancer cells, but instead they stimulated the body's immune response to fight off the cancer itself.

The article also covered human case studies. One report from Korea claimed that after ingesting *P. linteus* for 18 months, a 65-year-old man's hepatocellular carcinoma spontaneously regressed. Another report from Japan claimed that P. linteus had positive effects on a cancer patient with progressive bone metastasis. The most promising case study came from a 79-year-old man who took a *P. linteus* extract for 1 month without any other treatment. After six months, his lung cancer completely regressed.

Case Study 2

In the September 2007 issue of Positive Health Magazine, nutritionist and chef Dale Pinnock highlighted a patient who had positive experiences with medicinal mushrooms. The 23-year-old female patient came to his practice, looking for relief from her yearly bout of hay-fever. The symptoms came every summer and included stinging watery eyes, sinus blockage and pain, dry throat, and headaches. Once the summer season started, her symptoms persisted until cool weather hit in fall. The only relief she received was when it rained, and the pollen counts were lower. She had attempted to use a variety of aids, including antihistamines, pharmaceutical and natural anti-inflammatories, and herbal tonics. Nothing provided relief for more than a few hours, and many of the medicines stopped providing relief after a few weeks of use. The patient had moved around the globe at a young age, so she was not used to the types of pollen present in her new home country.

Based on Mr. Pinnock's and other practitioners' past success with medicinal mushrooms, he decided to prescribe reishi mushroom (*Ganoderma lucidum*) to the patient. The choice of reishi mushroom was made based on the evidence that polysaccharides found in the species could produce immune boosting responses in the body. The prescription was based upon 1000 mg reishi tablets. They were taken in doses of two tablets at three times per day.

During the first two days of treatment, the patient's symptoms became stronger. But on day three, the patient was able to wake up and breath through her nose for the first time in six weeks. Her eyes remained comfortable throughout most of the day, a stark contrast to the past few weeks of persistent discomfort. By the end of the first week of treatment, the patient was basically asymptomatic. After one month, the patient returned and reported many positive changes in her life. Most notable was the ability to sit and enjoy the outdoors in the summertime, a task which was impossible for the patient for years.

Case Study 3

A recent publication, _Ganoderma lucidum (Reishi mushroom) for cancer treatment_ by Xingzhong Jin and others, explored the benefits of the reishi mushroom. They collected as much information as they could by searching scientific databases, analyzing past lab trials, and consulting with herbal medicine experts and manufacturers. The initial study was performed in October 2011 with updates being provided in February 2016. The objective of the study was "to evaluate the clinical effects of G. lucidum on long-term survival, tumor response, host immune functions and quality of life in cancer patients, as well as adverse events associated with its use."

By analyzing 5 randomized controlled trials, they were able to conclude that G. _lucidum_ does not have the evidence to be singly used for cancer treatment. However, they did recommend that G. _lucidum_ could be administered alongside conventional treatment, such as chemotherapy or radiation therapy. One important note was that four out of the five studies had shown improved quality of life in patients receiving G. _lucidum_ during conventional treatment. Mild side effects were only noted in one of the five trials, with some nausea and insomnia being present. Their cautious recommendation was influenced by their analysis of the methodological quality of the trials, which they deemed to be inadequate. Their final advice was that future clinical research needs to be performed with higher quality to determine the effects of G. _lucidum_ on long-term cancer survival.

30

The Mushrooms

Agaricus bisporus

Agaricus bisporus, commonly known as white mushroom, button mushroom, baby bella, cremini, portabella, common mushroom, and a host of other names. It is the most widely cultivated mushroom in the world, with production active in at least 70 countries. In the USA, it is the most widely available mushroom and is a common site at supermarkets.

The mushroom is sold in many different forms, leading to the plethora of different names. When the fruiting bodies are small and brown, they are referred to as cremini or baby bella. When these brown mushrooms are allowed to mature and grow into larger caps, they are referred to as portabella. When the mushrooms are white, they are referred to as button or white mushrooms. Originally, the mushrooms were always brown, but a genetic mutation in a few mushrooms was isolated and cultivated, as the white color was seen as a more attractive food.

While *A. bisporus* is not necessarily known for any outstanding medicinal effects, some research has been conducted regarding the nutritional value and preventative care related to eating mushrooms. Recently, a case study investigated the diets of a large group of over 2,000 women, approximately half of whom had been diagnosed with breast cancer. The study found that women who consumed more than 10 grams of fresh mushrooms daily had a lower chance of developing breast cancer. The women who consumed mushrooms and green tea daily had more than an 80% decrease in their risk of breast cancer. A similar study was performed with over 300 Korean women with similar findings. Mushroom consumption was inversely proportional with the incidence of breast cancer.

Agaricus blazei

Agaricus blazei is commonly known as the almond mushroom, mushroom of life, himematsutake, and other names. It has been classified under a few scientific names, such as Agaricus brasiliensis and Agaricus rufotegulis. The mushrooms are edible and have a sweet, almond-like taste and smell. The species is native to Brazil and enjoys worldwide consumption and cultivation, especially in Brazil, Japan, and China.

Mushroom caps from A. blazei can grow from 2 to 7 inches across. As the caps begin to form, they feature silky hairs. As they mature, the caps develop small scales. The surface color can range from white to gray to reddish brown. The internal flesh of A. blazei is white and the flavor has been described as "green nuts". The stems are anywhere from 2.5 to 6 inches in height and around .5 inches thick. The stems are hollow when mature and include a bulb at the base. The gills start out white and gradually change to a blackish brown, caused by the dark purple coloring of the mature spores.

A. blazei has shown promising health benefits in lab and clinical studies. It has been used as a form of treatment for diabetes, cancer, dermatitis, hepatitis, arteriosclerosis, and other ailments. While human studies are limited, they have been performed in recent years. Some studies have shown that extracts from *A. blazei* can improve insulin resistance in diabetic patients, while also reducing cholesterol, weight, and body fat in able-bodied people. Patients with ulcerative colitis, an inflammatory bowel disease, have seen improved quality of life when consuming *A. blazei*. Another study showed improved liver function in Hepatitis B patients that consumed *A. Blazei*.

Other studies have explored the effects of *A. blazei* and cancer treatment. For instance, data from one study showed that a daily dose of *A. blazei* can improve cancer remissions patients' quality of life. While not yet touted as a cancer "cure" in any way, myeloma patients that have taken extracts of *A. blazei* have benefited from the immunomodulatory effects of the fungus. Normally, a range of pharmaceutical drugs are used as immunomodulators, but these drugs can have serious side effects. Thalidomide, lenalidomide, and pomalidomide are currently used for this purpose, and various side effects such as birth defects, skin irritation, and burning sensations have been recorded.

Some scientists have expressed caution about *A. blazei*, citing data that some laboratory samples of the fungus have shown high levels of inorganic arsenic. However, this could be due to a variety of reasons, most notably that many mushrooms consume toxic metals if they are found in their growing environment. As always, make sure that your medicinal mushrooms come from a reliable source to ensure clean, nutritious samples.

Recently, a few companies have attempted to capitalize on the popularity of *A. blazei* by marketing their products with information on the labels regarding many of the studies mentioned above. As a result, the U.S. Food and Drug Administration has sent warning letters to many of these companies, claiming that the mushroom products are "not generally recognized as safe and effective for the referenced uses". If the FDA had the best interests of human health in mind, they might spend more of their money and efforts on medicinal mushroom research, rather than hassling companies over the semantics of their packaging.

Auricularia auricula-judae

Auricularia auricula-judae is commonly known as Jew's ear, wood ear, jelly ear, or other names. The mushroom grows worldwide on dead or living wood, usually on elder trees. The name "Jew's ear" is a shortened version of the old common name for the mushroom, "Judas' ear". The name is derived from the story of Judas Iscariot, one of the Twelve Apostles of Jesus Christ, and his suicide by hanging from an elder tree. Species of *Auricularia* are thought to be the first mushroom that was cultivated, rather than foraged, in China around 600 AD.

The fruiting bodies of *A. auricula-judae* are usually around one to three inches across. The wood ear mushrooms get their name from their unusual shape which tends to resemble a large human ear.

Fresh specimens are tough and rubbery, while the dried mushrooms are hard and crisp. The color can vary and ranges from red to brown to purple. As a wood ear matures, it will usually gain folds and wrinkles which lends to its "ear" appearance. The fungi can be found in nature or cultivated on wood logs or sawdust.

A. auricula-judae is a "jelly" type fungus that is revered in Asian cooking for its crunchy and rubbery texture. In modern times, the fungi has become a food of interest for the elderly, as it contains high levels of polysaccharides that have been shown to help defend against Alzheimer's disease.

A. auricula-judae has a history of use in folk medicine dating back to the 16th century. Herbalist John Gerard wrote about the mushroom's use as a cure for sore throats. In his writings from 1597, he outlined a recipe for a liquid extract that involved boiling wood ear mushrooms in milk or steeping them in beer. The resulting liquid would then be consumed to heal a sore throat. In 1694, herbalist John Pechey described using the mushroom as a poultice to treat eye diseases and inflammation.

Recent research has found that A. auricula-judae contains glucans that exhibit strong anti-tumor properties when given to mice with sarcoma tumors. In similar studies, diabetic mice were giving a polysaccharide derived from wood ear mushrooms. The compound had a hypoglycemic effect on the mice and helped regulate their insulin, glucose, and food intake levels. A different polysaccharide was extracted from the mushrooms and shown to have blood thinning and anticoagulant properties.

Boletus edulis

Boletus edulis, also known as cepe, penny bun, porcini, or just "bolete", is an edible mushroom that has worldwide distribution and appreciation. The species can be found across Europe, North America, and Asia. It does not have natural distribution in the Southern Hemisphere. It prefers cool temperatures and sub-tropical regions. The name "porcini" comes from Italian, where local folklore believes that the mushrooms sprout when a new moon takes place.

The cap of the mushroom is usually a reddish-brown wine color that spans anywhere from 3 to 12 inches. The stem can be 3 to 10 inches in height and up to 3 inches thick, giving the bolete mushrooms their characteristic short and stout appearance. *B. edulis* is a great edible species to hunt for, as there are limited poisonous look-alikes that are relatively easy to differentiate from the real thing.

B. edulis is mycorrhizal, meaning the fungus creates a mutually beneficial relationship with specific plants. For instance, *B. edulis* can be found in mycorrhizal relationships with the Chinese chestnut tree. The fungus reduces the stress caused by lack of water for the tree, while also increasing leaf production and water-holding capabilities. A "hartig net" is often formed between *B. edulis* and the roots of trees and plants. The mycelium will grow around nutrient-absorbing tips of a plant's roots, allowing for the exchange of nutrients between the two species. In essence, this expands the root system of a host plant to the size of the symbiotic fungi. There are over 25 known host plants for *B. edulis*, including Chinese red pine, Coast Douglas-fir, mountain pine, and Virginia pine. Similarly, the mushroom has been found to grow alongside *Amanita muscaria,* the popular red and white mushroom known for its hallucinogenic effects. However, scientists are unsure if this due to similar ideal conditions between the two or a true mycorrhizal relationship.

Bolete mushrooms are a popular edible mushroom found in kitchens worldwide. They are especially popular in Europe in countries such as Italy, France, Germany, and Poland. If collecting wild specimens, caution should be taken and the site of picking should be noted. *B. edulis* is known to tolerate and consume heavy metals in the environment, such as mercury, cadmium, caesium, and others. Not only can they be dried for long term use, but they are one of the few mushrooms that are pickled and canned, leading to their year-round use. Bolete mushrooms have an estimated nutrient content of 7% proteins, 3% fats, and 9% carbohydrates, depending on the individual mushroom and growing conditions. The mushrooms have an earthy, nutty, or meaty flavor and are often paired with beef dishes, hearty stews, and egg omelets. Due to their history of Italian use and appreciation, porcini risotto is a popular dish that is traditionally eaten in the fall in Italy. A recipe for this dish can be found in the "recipes" section of this book.

Bolete mushrooms are not only edible, but they provide medicinal value as well. Traditional Chinese medicine has used the fungus for leg pain, limb numbness, discomfort in bones and tendons, and other ailments. Recent studies with extracts of the mushrooms have been shown to have anti-tumor properties in mice. In one study, the compounds were shown to have a 100% inhibition rate against sarcoma cells implanted in the mice.

Cordyceps militaris

Cordyceps militaris, commonly known simply as *Cordyceps*, is a "entomopathogenic" fungus, meaning it is parasitic and attacks insect hosts. It is relatively common throughout the northern hemisphere and usually fruits between August and November. In North America, it is widely distributed but more common to the east of the Rocky Mountains. *C. militaris* is usually found victimizing the pupa or larva of butterflies and moths. The fungus attacks the underground larva, allowing the species to form a club-like fruiting body that emerges out of the ground and spreads its spores to other insects. There are many varieties of Cordyceps that attack different insects, but *C. militaris* and *Ophiocordyceps sinensis* have been explored the most for their medicinal benefits. A relative of *C. militaris*, *Cordyceps lloydii*, has evolved to attack ants and secrete a chemical that motivates them to climb to the top of a tree and die, allowing the mushroom to grow out of the ant's head and spread the spores into the winds.

The fruiting bodies of *C. militaris* range from 1 to 3 inches long and are about 1/4 inch in width. The mushrooms range in color from pure orange to a paler, whiter orange color. The upper portion of the fruiting bodies are bumpy and pimply, while the lower half is smooth and narrows at the base.

Many studies have explored the myriad of benefits that *C. militaris* has the potential to offer. One such study explored the effects of polysaccharides found in *C. militaris* and their effects on exercise and fatigue. In the 28-day study, mice who received the polysaccharides were able to swim longer than the control group, leading to the suggestion that C. militaris may be useful for fatigue resistance. Another study suggested that small amounts of *C. militaris* may improve tolerance to high intensity exercise, while the benefits could be compounded with higher doses.

Additionally, the anti-aging and antioxidant effects of *C. militaris* have been explored. In lab studies, polysaccharides found in C. militaris inhibited mitochondrial swelling and increased the activities of different antioxidants.

In test tube studies, extracts of *C. militaris* have been shown to have cytotoxic (cell-killing) effects on different types of cancer cells found in humans, including lung, skin, liver, and colon cancers. Additionally, a variety of species of *Cordyceps*, including *C. militaris*, have exhibited anti-tumor effects on mice implanted with lymphoma, melanoma, and lung cancer. Varieties of *Cordyceps* may be able to reverse the negative side effects associated with cancer therapies like radiation and chemotherapy. One side effect in particular, leukopenia, causes the number of white blood cells to decrease, slowing the body's natural defense system and increasing the risk of infection. In one study, mice were given radiation and chemotherapy drugs. Some mice developed leukopenia, which was then reversed by the administration of *Cordyceps* on said mice.

A variety of *Cordyceps* species have been shown to have beneficial effects on cholesterol levels. Higher cholesterol levels have often suggested poor heart health and an increased risk of heart disease. Research in rodents has suggested that *Cordyceps* may decrease LDL cholesterol, also known as the "bad" cholesterol. LDL raises the risk of heart disease, due to its tendency to cause a buildup of cholesterol in the arteries. In a similar study, *C. militaris* was found to decrease triglyceride levels in mice and hamsters. Triglycerides are a type of fat found in your blood and high levels are another indicator of poor health and heart disease risk.

Flammulina velutipes

Flammulina velutipes, commonly known as enokitake or velvet shank, is a common culinary mushroom that also contains significant medicinal benefits. The mushroom is one of the earliest to be cultivated by humans, around the year 800 AD. *F. velutipes* enjoys cold weather and usually fruits in late fall or winter.

The mushrooms caps range in size from 0.5 to 3 inches across, while the stems range in height from 1 to 4 inches. The orange to red cap has a rubbery or sticky feel to it, while the stem has the velvety texture that earns the species it's nickname. The stem will often have a gradient, growing darker as it moves closer to the cap. *F. velutipes* can be found growing from hardwoods. The fungus is sometimes found to be terrestrial, but that is usually an optical illusion caused by buried hardwood.

In 1993, *F. velutipes* was used in a space study to determine the viability of the mushrooms in low gravity. Cultures of the fungus were carried on board the Space Shuttle Columbia and fruiting was induced. Normally, the mushrooms grow "upwards", with the caps being more or less parallel to the ground. In the study, the space mushrooms didn't have gravity to tell them which way was up, so they fruited at all angles from the substrate.

In 2001, a study was published regarding around 175,000 inhabitants of the Nagano region of Japan, a popular area for *F. velutipes* cultivation. The study covered a 15-year period between 1972 and 1986, finding that farmers of *F. velutipes* had a 40% lower death rate than the general population. The study suggested that this was caused by the farmers' increased consumption of *F. velutipes*.

Fomes fomentarius

Fomes fomentarius, commonly known as hoof fungus, tinder fungus, or ice man fungus, is a polypore fungus that takes the shape of a hoof as it grows. "Ice man fungus" refers to Ötzi, who was a man that was frozen in a glacier for around 5000 years until his discovery in 1991. Among his belongings were two mushroom species, one of which was *F. fomentarius*. Scientists believe he was using it as tinder to aid in fire starting. The fungus is perennial with some specimens surviving for up to thirty years.

F. fomentarius is found on the wood of hardwoods, including birch and beech. The fungus is parasitic and causes white rot in the trees that it inhabits. The conks produced by F. fomentarius can range in size from 2 to over 15 inches across, while being anywhere from 1 to 10 inches thick. The surface of the fruiting bodies is tough and woody, while the inside flesh is hard and fibrous. The color can have a wide range, and specimens ranging from white to black have been found. As the mushroom matures, it develops a hard "cuticle" layer that makes it difficult to process into usable forms.

Tinder fungus is one of the main mushrooms used to create amadou, a spongy fire-starting material used for centuries by humans. This is the substance that Ötzi the Ice Man had in his possession. To prepare amadou, fresh mushrooms are boiled and beaten into a leather-like substance. Amadou not only has excellent fire-starting properties, but it can also be used for its water absorbing abilities and astringent properties. Fly fishermen often use amadou to dry their artificial flies before storage. In the past, dentists used amadou to dry out teeth, while surgeons have used it to stop bleeding.

F. fomentarius has been studied for its effects on cancer. One such study successfully used extracts of the fungus to limit the growth of cancer cells in mice that were implanted with sarcoma, a form of cancer. Similarly, another study used *F. fomentarius* to successfully slow down and kill human breast cell cancers. This was done in a lab environment with "cultured cell lines", as opposed to a human clinical trial.

Extracts of *F. fomentarius* have been tested for use against the herpes simplex virus. The fungus had beneficial effects on the virus, even at dosages that are safe for human consumption.

Fomitopsis pinicola

Fomitopsis pinicola, commonly known as the red-belted conk or red-belted polypore, is found in coniferous forests in temperate regions of the Northern Hemisphere, especially Europe and Asia. It is usually saprobic, earning a reputation as a prolific decomposer and nutrient cycler, although it can sometimes be found on living trees as well. *F. pinicola* is a major producer of brown rot residues, an important component of soil in coniferous forests. The conks have a tough and woody feel. The cap surfaces have a glazed appearance and can vary in color from reddish brown to white and yellow. When sliced open, the inside flesh is white and leathery. The caps can grow to be around 16 inches across and 4 inches deep. The fungus is perennial and grows a new tube layer annually. Freshly gathered specimens may have a strong, musty odor.

In several central European countries, traditional medicine used *F. pinicola* for the treatment of bladder diseases, cancer, hemorrhoids, rheumatism, and other diseases.

Milkcoagulating and fibrinolytic activities in *F. pinicola* have also been detected. Because of these activities, scientists have concluded that medicinal mushrooms may be considered alternative natural sources to develop new pharmaceuticals with thrombolytic/fibrinolytic effects (blood clot prevention/treatment). *F. pinicola* is of particular interest to scientists for other treatments because it contains no toxic side effects, determined by lab tests and thousands of years of use. However, lab research has been limited and needs to be explored further. Multiple publications report that compounds in F. *pinicola* are promising for possible anti-cancer and anti-inflammatory effects, but more research would need to be done to conclude those findings.

Ganoderma lucidum

Ganoderma lucidum is one of the most popular medicinal mushrooms. It has a long history of use in China, Japan, and other Asian countries. It is commonly referred to as reishi, which is the Japanese name for the mushroom. In China, the *G. lucidum* is known as lingzhi. It is unofficially called the "The Mushroom of Immortality", referring to its many purported health benefits.

G. lucidum is named after the Latin word lucidus, which means "shiny" or "brilliant". This name refers to the glossy appearance of the mushroom's surface. Reishi mushrooms have a woody texture which makes them generally unfavorable to eat without further preparation. However, they are not poisonous, nor do they have any poisonous look-alikes.

There are a few colors and varieties of reishi mushrooms, including red, black, and green. These different varieties are often classified differently, such as *G. sinense* for the black and purple varieties.

44

While these mushrooms are similar and sometimes interchangeable, we will be referring to and talking about the red reishi, or *G. lucidum*, which is the most widely used and cultivated of the different varieties. Many mycologists believe that the related *Ganoderma* species are the same for most intents and purposes, with the main differences being habitat, location, and color.

Reishi has been documented as a medicinal mushroom for over 2,000 years. Due to the rarity of wild reishi, it was originally a luxurious mushroom that only the nobility could afford. This rarity may have contributed to the mysticism and claims of immortality that have surrounded *G. lucidum* since ancient times. These days, it is widely cultivated and available around the globe.

Although limited clinical studies have been made, there is strong evidence that reishi mushrooms have antioxidant properties and may enhance immune response. There are many further claims and beliefs, such as that *G. lucidum* can help slow and stop the spread of cancer. However, these are mostly based on anecdotal evidence and traditional use, so they should be taken with a grain of salt.

Traditional Chinese medicine uses reishi mushrooms to aid a variety of health conditions. Reishi has been used to stop respiratory issues such as coughing, wheezing, and phlegm. It has also been used for general preventative care and to strengthen "qi", which is the circulating life force often referred to in Chinese medicine.

Reishi mushrooms contain beta-glucans, a complex sugar that has been shown to stop the spread and growth of cancer cells in lab studies. In the studies, the immune systems of lab animals became more active when introduced to beta-glucans. Another substance found in reishi, triterpenes, may help lower blood pressure and prevent allergies. Triterpenes are especially high in the spores, as oil made from the spores can contain over 30% triterpines. The mushrooms have also been used to slow blood clotting. The results of animal lab studies and several human studies suggest that *G. lucidum* can help normalize blood glucose and cholesterol levels.

Several new compounds isolated from reishi mushrooms, including triterpenoids and lucidenic acids, were suggested as promising bioactive agents for the treatment of metabolic syndrome, which is a group of conditions that increase the risk of heart disease, stroke, and diabetes.

G. lucidum may play an important role in cancer treatment, where some medicinal mushrooms are already being used alongside modern Western medicine. In one study of about 4,000 breast cancer survivors, 58.8% of the women reported frequent use of G. lucidum. The researchers concluded that this post-survival G. lucidum was associated with "better social well-being". Several in vitro (test tube) studies have shown reishi's effectiveness in killing cancer cells. Another in vitro study showed that polysaccharides derived from reishi mushrooms inhibited the growth of prostate cancer cells, with the researchers suggesting that the polysaccharides may have potential in the treatment and prevention of prostate cancer. However, there has not been many animal or human trials to confirm these cancer-killing findings.

One 2016 survey analyzed 5 randomized controlled trials. Their conclusion that G. lucidum does not have the evidence to be singly used for cancer treatment. However, they did recommend that G. lucidum could be administered alongside conventional treatment, such as chemotherapy or radiation therapy. One important note was that four out of the five studies had shown improved quality of life in patients receiving G. lucidum during conventional treatment. Mild side effects were only noted in one of the five trials, with some nausea and insomnia being present. Their cautious recommendation was influenced by their analysis of the methodological quality of the trials, which they deemed to be inadequate. Their final recommendation was that future clinical research needs to be performed with higher quality to determine the effects of G. lucidum on long-term cancer survival.

Reishi mushrooms have also been shown to be effective against depression and fatigue. One study analyzed over 130 people with neurasthenia, a medical condition associated with emotional disturbance that causes fatigue, headaches, and irritability. The research found that the patients who were administered with G. lucidum had a greater sense of well-being and a decrease in fatigue. The researchers concluded that reishi mushroom had better results than a placebo in improving the symptoms associated with neurasthenia. A similar study covered a group of almost 50 breast cancer survivors. The women who received reishi mushroom powder over 4 weeks had reduced fatigue and improved quality of life versus a control group.

Because of the wide variety of effects that G. lucidum has been shown to have, the species is often considered an "adaptogen". This means it can fill a wide variety of roles in the body and can seemingly 'adapt' to what the body needs.

Grifola frondosa

Grifola frondosa, commonly referred to as maitake, is a popular medicinal mushroom with many benefits that have been explored in traditional cultures and modern science. The name "maitake" comes from the Japanese terms mai, meaning "dance", and take, which translates to "mushroom". It is also called hen-of-the-woods, ram's head, and sheep's head.

G. frondosa makes its home at the base of oak, elm, and maple trees in areas of Japan, China, and North America. It is a perennial fungus, and the mycelium will often produce fruiting bodies for a few years in a row. The mushroom caps usually grow in large clusters that can grow to over 50 inches in size. Each individual cap is around one to four inches and grayish-brown in color. The stalk becomes tough and branch-like as the mushroom matures. There are a few toxic look-alikes, so be careful if harvesting wild mushrooms, as always.

In China and Japan, maitake mushrooms have been eaten as food for centuries and make up a large portion of the culinary mushroom industry. It is commonly used in the Japanese dish "Nabemono", which is a hot, soupy dish also called "one pot" or "things in a pot".

The mushroom is often referred to as an "adaptogen", meaning it serves a wide array of functions in the body and can seemingly adapt to whatever the body needs.

In East Asian countries such as China, Taiwan, and Japan, maitake has a history of use in aiding a variety of health conditions, including arthritis, hepatitis, and HIV. Traditional Chinese medicine has also used it to enhance the immune system.

Recent studies have been exploring the mushroom's effects on the immune system and tumors. Similar to many other medicinal mushrooms, maitake contains a potent polysaccharide that has been shown to have anti-tumor effects on lab animals. The polysaccharides found in maitake are thought to be different or more powerful than other mushrooms.

Clinical studies have been performed with humans to judge the mushroom's effect on cancer therapy. In a study featuring 165 patients, 90% of the people reported that their cancer-related issues had improved, such as hair loss and nausea. In addition, 83% of the patients expressed a reduction in pain. Other clinical studies have shown increases in the immunological functions of cancer patients. The results of animal lab studies and several human studies suggest that *G. frondosa* can help normalize blood glucose and cholesterol levels.

Multiple studies have been made to determine the effects of *G. frondosa* on obesity. In a lab study, overweight rats were given a daily dose of maitake in powder form. These rats lost more weight than the control group over 18 weeks. In a similar observational study with humans, patients were given maitake tablets every day for two months. Thirty of the patients reported a loss in weight of up to 26 pounds. However, this was an uncontrolled study and should be taken with a grain of salt.

Geastrum triplex

Geastrum triplex is also known as earthstar, "stomach fungi", or collared earthstar. The *Geastrum* genus of fungi have a unique appearance and functionality. Rather than a traditional stem and cap, earthstar fruiting bodies feature a spore-filled sac that looks like a stomach. This sac then opens up to reveal the star shape that earns the species its nickname. The sac is usually around .5 to 2 inches wide, while the opened-up earthstars are around 2 to 4 inches across.

The skin, also known as the peridium, of the mushrooms are made of three layers. Young earthstar mushrooms are shaped like an onion. When rain hits the mushroom, the outer two layers split and curl away from the center, forming a star shape with up to a dozen rays. These star rays lift the mushroom off the ground to be clear of debris. Sometimes, the rays push high enough to disconnect from the mycelium and seemingly "walk", albeit very slowly. After the inner sac wears away from the rain, spores are released into the air to start the life cycle all over again.

In traditional Chinese medicine, earthstar mushrooms have been used to reduce respiratory tract inflammation. They have also been used to reduce swelling and staunch blood flow from wounds. There has not been much modern research into the medicinal effects of *G. triplex*.

When the fresh stars are harvested and dried, they can make for an excellent ornamental decoration.

Hericium erinaceus

Hericium erinaceus, commonly known as lion's mane, boasts one of the more unusual fruiting bodies in the medicinal mushroom world. The fruiting body is white throughout, with a large clump of long spines that look like melting icicles or a lion's mane. The mushroom ranges in size from 3 to 7 inches across and usually shows up in the wounds of living hardwood trees. The species enjoys a wide distribution across North America and fruits in late summer to fall in most areas. Warmer climates promote fruiting in the winter or spring seasons.

The medicinal benefits of *H. erinaceus* have been explored by modern scientists, especially in the fields of brain and nerve health. In conjunction with other mushrooms, lion's mane are used in the production of functional foods for the prevention and treatment of diabetes. Compounds found in *H. erinaceus* may have positive effects on brain health and are being considered for use in the treatment or management of depression, Alzheimer's, Huntington's, and Parkinson's diseases. The brain healing effect has mainly been attributed to the discovery of various "terpenoids" that stimulate the production of nerve growth factor (NGF), a substance that is integral to the health of the central nervous system. Experimental studies have shown that polysaccharides and terpenoids found in the fruiting bodies and mycelium of *H. erinaceus* can stimulate the synthesis of NGF, promote the growth and differentiation of neurons in the brain, and protect cells against oxidative stress. Various species of *Hericium* are praised for their production of bioactive compounds that can be used for treatment of neurodegenerative diseases.

Numerous bioactive compounds derived from *H. erinaceus* have been developed into food supplements and alternative medicines. A placebo-controlled trial was performed on Japanese men and women diagnosed with mild cognitive impairment. The patients were given 250 mg tablets containing *H. erinaceus* powder three times a day for 16 weeks. The results of the study concluded that *H. erinaceus* is effective in improving mild cognitive impairment.

The results of animal lab studies and several human studies suggest that *H. erinaceus* can help normalize blood glucose and cholesterol levels.

H. pylori is a common type of bacteria that grows in the digestive tract. It tends to attack the stomach lining, with cases usually showing up in children. It infects the stomachs of roughly 60% of the world's adult population. While *H. pylori* infections are usually harmless, they are also responsible for the majority of ulcers in the stomach and small intestine. Recently, a randomized trial of 25 patients compared the usefulness of *H. erinaceus* and essential oils against *H. pylori* infection. The study revealed that patients who received *H. erinaceus* tested negative for *H. pylori* in 89.5% of cases, while only 33.3% of patients tested negative after being treated with essential oils. The study concluded that H. *erinaceus* could be considered an alternative to antibiotic therapy against *H. pylori* and its associated diseases.

Inonotus obliquus

Inonotus obliquus, commonly known as chaga, has a history of folk medicine use in places such as Russia, Poland, and most of the Baltic countries. It goes by a few other names, including black mass, clinker polypore, birch canker, and cinder conk. Today, the mushroom has gained popularity in the Western world due to its perceived health benefits.

I. obliquus grows in cold climates, such as Northern Europe, Russia, Northern Canada, and other locations. It is usually found on the bark of birch trees. The fruiting body of *I. obliquus,* also called a conk, is a woody growth that looks similar to a lump of charcoal. The inside of the mushroom contains a soft, orange colored core. The growth can be up to 12 inches across.

Traditional consumption involved processing chaga into a fine powder and brewing it as an herbal tea. In traditional medicine, the mushroom has been used to treat diabetes, cancerous tumors, and heart disease. Studies of a "polyphenolic extract" from the mushroom have indicated that the mushroom has strong antioxidant properties.

One study explored the immunomodulatory effects of *I. obliquus*. They concluded that chaga is a strong immune modulator that can help the bone marrow system recover after being damaged by chemotherapy. The researchers also suggested that extracts of *I. obliquus* show potential for use as a supplement or therapeutic for people with compromised immune systems that have experienced bone marrow system damage.

Other studies have looked at chaga's effects on tumors. One such *in vitro* (test tube) study demonstrated that extracts of *I. obliquus* could be used to inhibit the growth of tumors and kill existing cancerous cells. Another study was conducted that involved lab mice. Some mice were given extracts of *I. obliquus* for 3 weeks prior to being implanted with tumors. These mice experienced less tumor growth and a maintenance of body temperature. Additionally, the mice lost body weight. The researchers concluded that *I. obliquus* has the potential to be used as a natural cancer treatment and for general health care.

Another *in vitro* study demonstrated that extracts from *I. obliquus* have strong cytotoxic (cell-killing) against both mouse breast cancer cells and human breast cancer cells. They quote this as having to do with the triterpenes present in the fungus.

Other studies have explored the effects of *I. obliquus* on diabetes. Multiple experiments with mice have determined that chaga has the potential to regulate blood sugar levels. One group of mice that were fed extracts of I. *obliquus* over 3 weeks experienced over 10% reductions in their blood glucose levels.

One study with mice showed that extracts from chaga can reduce inflammation and damage in the gut by inhibiting inflammatory proteins.

Lentinula edodes

Lentinula edodes, commonly known as Shiitake, has been consumed in China, Japan, and other Asian countries for thousands of years. While the mushroom has been widely consumed as a nutritious food, it has also been shown to provide medicinal benefits.

The Shiitake mushroom is one of the most widely cultivated and consumed mushrooms in the world. The fungi are usually found in tropical and subtropical regions and make their home on the deadwood of broad-leaved trees. The mushrooms are usually a shade of brown and can have a cap ranging in size from 1 to 10 inches. Shiitake mushrooms produce white spores.

Shiitake mushrooms are high in dietary fiber, B vitamins, iron, copper, and other important nutrients. They are known for their earthy flavor and provide an "umami" or savory flavor, which is one of the few basic tastes (the other being sweet, sour, bitter, and salt). When cooked, the caps of a shiitake mushroom have a meaty texture. The stems tend to be tough unless they are cooked longer.

L. edodes has been tested and shown to have anti-tumor properties in both animals and humans. This is due to a variety of chemicals present in the fungus, most notable of which is polysaccharide lentinan. Shiitake has also been demonstrated to be effective against many viruses and infections. Some research has even found *L. edodes* to be useful in the treatment of AIDS, inhibiting HIV infections. Some of these effects have been produced from different aspects of Shiitake, most notably the mycelium. *L. edodes* has been shown to have beneficial effects on lowering the levels of blood glucose, cholesterol, and arterial pressure in animal experiments.

Morchella esculenta

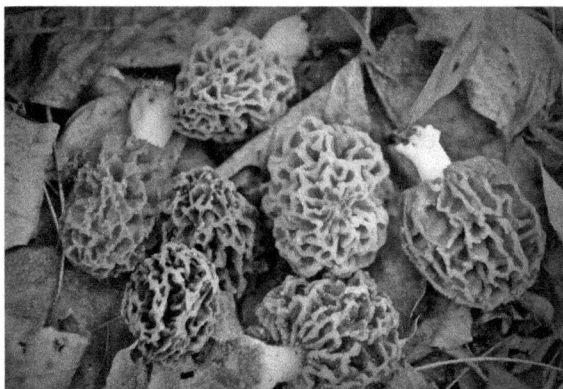

Morchella esculenta, commonly known as the yellow morel, true morel, or simply "morel", is one of the most recognizable and sought-after edible mushrooms in the world. The mushrooms are prized for their nutty and meaty flavor. This flavor comes to full effect when fried with butter, which is one of the most popular ways to cook them. Morel mushrooms must be cooked before eating because they contain hydrazine, a gastrointestinal irritant. The excitement and obsession with the mushroom have been amplified by the mushroom's inability to be domestically cultivated. Only recently have mycologists figured out the methods and conditions to successfully cultivate morels. The mushrooms pop up in the spring, leading to a yearly influx foraging for *M. esculenta*.

The fruiting bodies of *M. esculenta* have caps that are about 1.5 to 3 inches in width and 2 to 6 inches in height. The caps have a honeycomb pattern and are yellowish brown. The stems are usually around 1 to 2 inches in height and width. Slicing the mushrooms open reveals a completely hollow interior. Poisonous false morels include *Gyromitra caroliniana* and *Gyromitra brunnea*, which can be identified by a reddish color and a stalk that is not hollow. Another look-alike, the black morel, differs from a true morel by its black or dark brown colors. Occasionally, true morel mushrooms will have a hole bored in the top - be careful, as these may have centipedes living inside!

In traditional Chinese medicine, species of *Morchella* were used to treat indigestion, phlegm, and breathing issues.

The anti-inflammatory and antitumor properties of *M. esculenta* have been documented extensively. When extract of the cultured mycelium of *M. esculenta* was administered to mice with implanted tumors, the extracts exhibited significant antitumor activity. In the same study, the extract showed significant inhibition of both acute and chronic inflammation, comparable to the study's reference drug, Diclofenac.

A 2005 study helps confirm the antitumor results of the previously mentioned study. An extract of *M. esculenta* mycelium was orally administered to mice for 30 days, resulting in a 74% inhibition in tumor volume and a 79% decrease in tumor weight.

Other studies have raised concerns about the current methods of cultivation. The mushrooms are not often grown commercially, especially in less-developed countries. This has led to unsustainable harvesting practices that have negative effects on forest biodiversity and the surrounding ecosystem. Not only are the mushrooms overharvested, but people have actually been burning down forests and setting the ground on fire. This is due to the belief that morel mushrooms produce higher yields in areas that have previously been burned. Although this may be true, this has detrimental effects on the rest of the species in an area that is burned. Due to these realities, reliable domestic cultivation of *M. esculenta* is a highly researched topic.

Ophiocordyceps sinensis

Ophiocordyceps sinensis, commonly known as caterpillar fungus of simply "*Cordyceps*", is a parasitic fungus that lives and grows inside of ghost moth larvae. The spores germinate inside a living larva and kill it. The fungus then sends out a fruiting body from the corpse of its host. The fruiting bodies are dark brown or black and usually grow from 2 to 4 inches, longer than the caterpillar hosts. It is most commonly found in the highlands of Southwest China, Bhutan, and Nepal. Although it is not technically a mushroom, *O. sinensis* shares most of the same qualities of mushrooms and has been described as a "medicinal mushroom" in traditional Chinese medicine.

The fruiting body of *O. sinensis* is dark brown or black, while the host's body usually turns to a yellowish or brown color. The fruiting body grows a few centimeters out of the host and stands upright. In rural Tibet, the caterpillar fungus is a major source of income which has caused the species to become threatened from over harvesting. In 2008, one pound of the fungi could be sold for around $1,500 and up, with high quality specimens fetching over $5,000 per pound.

Traditional healers in Sikkim, a region of the Himalayas, recommend *O. sinensis* as an aid for "all illnesses". They claim that it can have positive effects on energy, stamina, endurance, libido, and sleep quality. It has the nickname "Himalayan Viagra" because of its libido enhancing properties. Apparently, the benefits of *O. sinensis* were discovered when grazing animals that ate the fungus became stronger and healthier.

Traditional Chinese medicine describes *O. sinensis* as sweet in taste and neutral in nature, claiming that it can replenish the kidney, soothe the lung, stop bleeding, and aid the respiratory system. According to the official Pharmacopoeia Commission of the People's Republic of China, the fungus has been used for the treatment of fatigue, kidney dysfunction, kidney failure, lethargy, and other conditions. *O. sinensis* is thought to have been first recorded in *Ben Cao Bei Yao*, a book written by Wang Ang in 1694 and has been used a natural remedy since at least that time. In China, over-harvesting and destruction of habitat has led to a decrease in yield of the fungus by over 90% in the past 25 years. This has caused prices to skyrocket and other varieties of Cordyceps, such as *C. militaris*, to gain recognition and use. It has since been discovered that many of these alternative Cordyceps species actually exhibit many of the same medicinal benefits.

Recently, a study conducted on lab mice tested if *O. sinensis* had an effect on endurance. After three weeks of consuming the fungus, the mice were able to swim significantly longer than the control groups that did not receive the supplement. The results were dependent on dose, as a lower dose inspired a 73% increase in endurance, while a higher dose only increased endurance by 30%. These studies confirm what traditional medicine has already known for centuries. In a similar study involving a group of 20 healthy elderly people, the subjects were either given doses of *O. sinensis* or a placebo. The group that received the fungus had improved measures of exercise performance, and the researchers suggested that *O. sinensis* "improves exercise performance and might contribute to wellness in healthy older subjects."

Experiments have indicated that *O. sinensis* has potential to aid diabetes in a variety of ways, including trigger the release of insulin, increase hepatic glucokinase, and increase sensitivity of cells to insulin. In a human clinical trial, 95% of diabetes patients treated with a daily dose of *O. sinensis* saw improvements in their blood sugar profile. Similarly, a study was conducted involving diabetic rats. Initially, the diabetic rats had much lower weight gain and higher blood glucose responses than a control group. Once the diabetic rats were administered doses of *Cordyceps*, their diabetes-induced weight loss and hyperglycemic tendencies were controlled. The study concludes that *Cordyceps* species have the potential to be a functional food for diabetic patients.

O. sinensis has shown a high degree of usefulness in improving treatment outcomes in cancer, mostly due to the presence of immune-modulating polysaccharides. Studies have reported that *O. sinensis* can cause cancer cell death in multiple forms of cancer, including oral, bladder, leukemia, melanoma, breast, and prostate. A variety of species of *Cordyceps*, including *O. sinensis,* have exhibited anti-tumor effects on mice implanted with lymphoma, melanoma, and lung cancer. Additionally, some varieties of *Cordyceps* may be able to reverse the negative side effects associated with cancer therapies like radiation and chemotherapy. One side effect in particular, leukopenia, causes the number of white blood cells to decrease, slowing the body's natural defense system and increasing the risk of infection. In one study, mice were given radiation and chemotherapy drugs. Some mice developed leukopenia, which was then reversed by the administration of Cordyceps on said mice.

The anti-aging effects of *O. sinensis* have been explored. In a study involving older mice and rats, extracts from *O. sinensis* were shown to have improved the brain function and antioxidative activity in the rodents, as well as promoting sexual function. A similar study showed that extracts of *O. sinensis* can extend the lifespan of mice reverse many age-related changes in the mice. They conclude that these findings support the traditional beliefs and uses that surround *O. sinensis*.

In a research paper that reviewed over 20 studies involving over 1,700 people with chronic kidney disease, it was found that those who took *O. sinensis* supplements were able to enjoy improved kidney function. However, the authors did add that some of these studies were of poor quality and further research is needed to expound upon these findings.

The positive effects of *O. sinensis* on heart health has been widely researched. In China, *O. sinensis* has been used to treat arrhythmia, a condition related to irregular and slow heartbeats. In a study involving rats with chronic kidney disease, administration of *O. sinensis* reduced injuries to the heart in these rats. Chronic kidney disease is known to cause heart injuries and can often lead to heart failure. The results of this study are promising, revealing the fungus as a possible preventative care for patients with chronic kidney disease.

Additionally, a variety of *Cordyceps* species have been shown to have beneficial effects on cholesterol levels. Higher cholesterol levels have often suggested poor heart health and an increased risk of heart disease. Research in rodents has suggested that Cordyceps may decrease LDL cholesterol, also known as the "bad" cholesterol. LDL raises the risk of heart disease, due to its tendency to cause a buildup of cholesterol in the arteries.

Phellinus linteus

Phellinus linteus, also known as song gen, sanghuang, and black hoof mushroom, is a perennial fungus that grows most prominently on the mulberry tree. It can also be found on other hardwoods, including the Chinese lacquer tree, oaks, and aspens. The fruiting body resembles a hoof and features a bitter taste. The cap color can range from dark brown to black. There is no stem, as the fruiting bodies grow as a "bracket" or "shelf" fungus, protruding directly from the side of a tree. The inside of *P. linteus* is tough and woody and is therefore inedible.

P. linteus is commonly used in traditional Korean medicine by brewing the mushroom into a tea. Traditional Chinese medicine has used *P. linteus* to treat a variety of ailments, including hemorrhage, hemostasis, and issues with female menstruation.

A variety of compounds have been explored in *P. linteus*, including polysaccharides, flavones, terpenes, steroids, and furans. These compounds have had a variety of effects in lab studies, including antitumor, antioxidant, immuno-modulating, hypoglycemic, and anti-inflammatory activities. The results of animal lab studies and several human studies suggest that *P. linteus* can help normalize blood glucose and cholesterol levels. In one study, an extract of *P. linteus* helped lower blood glucose levels in rats with diabetes, although the extract was not able to prevent the onset of diabetes.

The polysaccharides found in *P. linteus* have been shown to have immune boosting and cytotoxic properties. One study performed an experiment with mice that were implanted with melanoma cells. The mice that were treated with *P. linteus* survived significantly longer than control groups. One important note was that the compounds in *P. linteus* do not directly kill the cancer cells, but instead they stimulate the body's immune response to fight off the cancer itself. In another study, polysaccharides from *P. linteus* were used in conjunction with a lower than normal dose of a chemotherapy drug to combat colon cancer cells. The combination was effective, allowing for much less side effects from the potentially harmful chemotherapy drugs. It was also noted that the healthy, non-cancerous colon cells remained unharmed.

61

Test tube studies and animal studies have both shown that extracts of *P. linteus* can kill human prostate cancer cells. In the study with mice, human cancer cells were injected into the mice. While the fungus extract did not prevent tumor growth, it did slow the growth down.

Polysaccharides from *P. linteus* have been shown to provide positive immunomodulating activity. These polysaccharides have been successfully used to treat mice that were given an allergy-induced eczema. In test tube studies, *P. linteus* was found to be effective against multiple strains of antibiotic-resistant *Staphylococcus* (Staph) infections, meaning the fungus might have antibacterial uses.

One report from Korea claims that after ingesting *P. linteus* for 18 months, a 65 year old man's hepatocellular carcinoma spontaneously regressed. Another report from Japan claimed that P. linteus had positive effects on a cancer patient with progressive bone metastasis. The most promising case study came from a 79 year old man who took a *P. linteus* extract for 1 month without any other treatment. After six months, his lung cancer completely regressed.

Pleurotus ostreatus

Pleurotus ostreatus is commonly known as the oyster mushroom. It is a close cousin of the king oyster mushroom and goes by a few other names, including tree oyster, oyster shelf, straw mushroom, and hiratake. In Japanese, Hiratake translates to "flat mushroom".

Oyster mushrooms grow wild in subtropical and temperate forests around the world. They are often found on dead deciduous trees, slowly feeding on and decomposing the dead organic material. The oyster-shaped cap usually spans around two to ten inches with colors ranging from white to dark-brown. The spores are usually a light white to gray color, so a spore print is best taken on a dark background.

P. ostreatus was first cultivated in Germany in World War I to help sustain the army. The edible mushroom features a bittersweet aroma, similar to that of bitter almonds. This aroma and flavor are caused by benzaldehyde in the mushrooms. The mushrooms are best eaten when young, as the caps become tough and lose flavor as they mature. Oyster mushrooms do have a few poisonous look-alikes in the wild, including *Omphalotus nidiformis*, *Clitocybe dealbata*, and *Omphalotus olivascens*. Be extra cautious if hunting for them in the wild.

Oyster mushrooms are one of the most popular mushrooms in the world and can be found in the diets of humans everywhere. The majority of the world's mushrooms, including oysters, are produced in China. In domestic cultivation, the mushrooms are usually grown on a substrate of straw, grain, or hay that is held in large, clear plastic bags. Another popular form of cultivation is glass jar production, especially for non-commercial growing at home. The glass jar method allows for smaller grows and easy sterilization at home using a pressure cooker or steam bath.

Oyster mushrooms are a rich source of nutrients, including protein, vitamins, minerals, and fiber. They also contain selenium, an antioxidant that has been shown to protect the body's cells from free radicals and oxidative stress. The results of animal lab studies and several human studies suggest that different *Pleurotus* species can help normalize blood glucose and cholesterol levels.

Polyporus umbellatus

Polyporus umbellatus, commonly known as Umbrella polypore, is a "butt rot" fungi, inhabiting the bases of trees. The mushrooms emerge from the base and roots of hardwood trees and can be found in northern North America. The mushrooms grow in clusters up to 20 inches wide. The individual caps are about 0.5 to 2 inches in width and have a white and tan coloring. The clusters are known to reappear in the same location year after year. They are known to be both parasitic and saprobic, as they are able to be found on living and dead trees.

In one lab study, *P. umbellatus* was given to rats to determine its diuretic effects. Data was collected concerning the rats' urine contents and behavior that led the researchers to conclude that *P. umbellatus* may be an effective diuretic medicine. This confirms recommendations from traditional Chinese medicine that *P. umbellatus* is a fungus that can drain "dampness". Dampness is thought of as too much moisture in the body, whether that be excessive water retention, phlegm, mucus, loose bowels, or other conditions.

Schizophyllum commune

Schizophyllum commune, commonly known as gillies or split gills, are a rather unique example of a medicinal mushroom. They are one of the most common and widely distributed mushrooms in the world. They can be found on every continent, excluding Antarctica. The fruiting bodies have a fan shape and look like spongey coral. Split gill mushrooms vary in color from yellow to white to gray and can be anywhere from 0.5 to 2 inches wide. The caps are tough and leathery and do not have a stem. *S. commune* is relatively easy to identify in the wild, as the folds and ridges in its body create a unique appearance. It usually appears out of dead hardwood trees, but is occasionally found to be parasitic on living trees. Unlike most other mushroom species, the fruiting bodies of *S. commune* have the ability to dry out and rehydrate throughout the year. The mycelium only needs to produce one flush of mushrooms per year, which is helpful in dry areas or seasons. The cracks or "splits" in a split gill are caused by this constant drying out and rehydration.

In the Western world, especially the U.S. and Europe, *S. commune* is usually described and thought of as inedible. However, this is due to an unacquired taste rather than toxicity, as the fungus is widely consumed in Mexico and other areas in the tropics. The mushroom is popular as a culinary ingredient in different parts of India. In the state of Manipur, the mushroom, known as "kanglayen", is commonly added to a local pancake-like dish called "paaknam". It is also regularly consumed in the Indian state of Mizoram. Consumption in the tropics because fleshy mushrooms, such as shiitakes, quickly rot out in the hot and humid environment. *S. commune* stores better and provides a more consistent product.

The medicinal effects of *S. commune* have been studied extensively, mostly in lab studies involving animals. A beta-glucan, "schizophyllan" or "SPG", has been identified as a useful cancer treatment when combined with chemotherapy and radiation therapy. In mice implanted with tumors, SPG was shown to reduce the size of the tumors and extend survival time of the mice. The results were found by comparing the mushroom-treated mice with a control group of mice treated with only radiation. In similar studies, SPG was found to offer protective benefits to the bone marrow cells of mice that were receiving chemotherapy and radiation therapy. SPG was most effective against this radiation damage when given to the mice at the same time as radiation.

The schizophyllan (SPG) found in *S. commune* has also been explored for its possible protection against infections. SPG treatment demonstrated protective effects against bacterial infections in mice, such as *P. aeruginosa, S. aureus, E. coli, and K. pneumoniae*. Similarly, SPG has been effective in protecting mice and Kuruma prawn against viral infections. The mice and shrimp had increased survival rates and higher virus-cell-killing activity when given oral doses of SPG. This leads one to infer that medicinal mushrooms are not only effective in mammals, but invertebrates like shrimp as well.

S. commune is known for their interesting sexual diversity - the species contains over 28,000 different sexes! They have evolved this way to encourage genetic diversity and prevent sibling or relative mating. A given individual fungus is sexually compatible with 99.9% of other individuals.

Taiwanofungus camphoratus

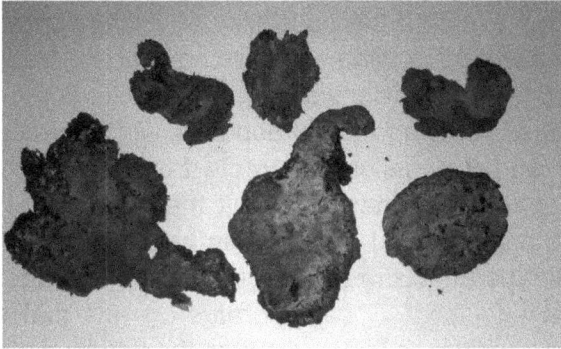

Taiwanofungus camphoratus, commonly known as stout camphor fungus, is endemic to Taiwan and the *Cinnamomum kanehirae* tree. The fungus has a couple of synonymous scientific names, including *Antrodia camphorata* and *Ganoderma camphoratum*. It is one of the highest valued medicinal mushrooms in Taiwan, although prices have gone down recently as domestication and indoor cultivation of the species has occurred. In 1997, high quality fruiting bodies were claimed to fetch over $5,000 per pound. Because of the popularity and high prices, overharvesting and illegal farming have led to negative effects on the host tree, *C. kanehirae.*

Traditional Taiwanese cultures used *T. camphoratus* to deal with alcohol toxicity and exhaustion. Traditional Chinese medicine used the mushroom for similar problems, including liver diseases, abdominal pain, and hypertension. *T. camphoratus* was not acknowledged and named by modern science until 1990.

In a lab study, novel compounds from *T. camphoratus* were isolated by submerging cultures in a solution. The compounds were then successfully used to inhibit the spread of tumor cells in vitro. Another study involved testing the fungus' anti-oxidant effects. The results were positive, and as the dose of T. camphoratus was raised, the "radical-scavenging" effect also followed. The results of the study suggested that *T. camphoratus* is a non-toxic antioxidant that could be added to health foods.

A 2008 review explored the possibility of *T. camphoratus* treating liver diseases and other ailments, building upon the traditional uses and knowledge from ancient cultures. Hepatitis B virus (HBV) is known to cause varying forms of hepatitis, which sometimes leads to cirrhosis and liver failure. Extracts from the mycelium of *T. camphoratus* were reported to inhibit the activities of HBV. The effects were compounded as the dose was increased. The study also explored the effects of the fungus on liver damage caused by alcohol. The effects of *T. camphoratus* on rats that were given alcohol were positive, as they prevented the negative effects on the liver. The effects were comparable to a common plant-extracted drug, silymarin.

Trametes versicolor

Trametes versicolor, commonly referred to as turkey tails, has been used for hundreds of years as medicine in traditional East Asian cultures. The "versicolor" name refers to the mushroom's radiating multi-colored designs, similar to that of a turkey's tail feathers. The conk ranges in size from one to four inches across and has a fuzzy or velvety feel to it. The insides of a turkey tail are white and rubbery. The spores of a turkey tail mushroom are white. The conks feature pores on the underside instead of gills.

Turkey tails are a "bracket" fungi and do not have a stem. The mushrooms usually grow on the sides of trees, including dead wood, living hardwood trees, and conifers. In the U.S., *T. versicolor* usually produces mushrooms from May through December, although some areas may experience year-round fruiting. They are known to be at their best in the fall and winter. While there are no known poisonous look-alikes of *T. versicolor*, caution should still be taken when attempting to identify a wild sample.

Due to their rough texture, fresh turkey tails are not usually eaten as food. After a fresh turkey tail has dried out, it can be ground up and brewed as a tea. The processed mushrooms can also be used in soups or as an addition to other meals.

Recently, studies have been made that point to *T. versicolor* having strong antioxidant and cytotoxic properties. Cytotoxic refers to the fungus' ability to attack and destroy cancer cells. Extracts of turkey tail mushrooms contain krestin (PSK) and polysaccharide peptide (PSP). Both polysaccharides are known to promote immune response and suppress inflammation. One *in vitro* (test tube) study concluded that the PSP found in turkey tails can increase a type of white blood cell called monocytes. These cells fight infection and boost immunity in the body.

In some East Asian countries, turkey tails are used alongside modern medicine to help fight cancer. A patient who undergoes surgery, chemotherapy, or radiation may also take extracts of turkey tail mushrooms due to their natural immune boosting properties. *T. versicolor* also has the ability to enhance gut health. The mushrooms contain prebiotics, which helps promote good gut bacteria. One study compared the effects of turkey tail mushrooms and amoxicillin (an antibiotic) on gut health. The study lasted 8 weeks and involved 24 healthy patients, each of which was given either a polysaccharide extract from *T. versicolor*, amoxicillin, or a placebo. The patients that received amoxicillin had substantial changes to their gut biome that took weeks to recover. The patients that received *T. versicolor* had "clear and consistent microbiome changes consistent with its activity as a prebiotic."

One publication reviewed 13 different studies that involved giving patients doses of turkey tail mushrooms alongside conventional cancer treatment. The study demonstrated that those with colorectal cancer, gastric cancer, or breast cancer had a 9% decrease in 5-year mortality rate compared to those who received chemotherapy alone. A similar review looked at 8 studies encompassing over 8,000 people who received PSK along with chemotherapy. The group that received PSK had a longer lifespan after surgery than the control group that received chemotherapy alone. Another study covered 11 women with breast cancer, some of which received a daily dose of turkey tail in powder form after each session of radiation therapy. The women who received the turkey tail showed an increase in the cancer fighting cells of the immune system, including natural killer cells and white blood cells.

Tremella fuciformis

Tremella fuciformis, commonly known as snow fungus, snow ear, silver ear fungus, and white jelly mushroom, produces gelatinous, jelly-like fruiting bodies. It is found in tropical and sub-tropical regions around the world, as well as a few parts of North America. *T. fuciformis* is closely associated and always found alongside another fungus, *Annulohypoxylon spp.* Mycologists have not determined whether *T. fuciformis* is parasitic upon the fungus, or if it forms a symbiotic relationship. The fruiting bodies of *T. fuciformis*

are translucent white and can grow to around 3 inches across and 2 inches high.

In traditional Chinese medicine, *T. fuciformis* was used as a beauty product for its anti-aging effects. One of the polysaccharides found in *T. fuciformis* has outstanding water retention abilities and can hold around 500 times its weight in water. This is much more than similar compounds used in modern beauty products, such as glycerin and hyaluronic. The white jelly mushroom has been applied topically by combining powdered extract of the mushroom with a carrier oil or lotion, such as coconut oil. Not only does the species promote soft and beautiful skin, but it promotes greater production of superoxide dismutase. This is an enzyme already created by the body and skin which serves as an antioxidant that can defend the skin from invading free radicals. *T. fuciformis* also contains significant levels of kojic acid, which can be used to smooth out inconsistencies in skin, such as freckles or dark spots.

Traditional Chinese medicine also used *T. fuciformis* in cough syrups and to treat respiratory illnesses. The water retention and hydrating abilities of the fungus make it useful for a variety of ailments. Studies have shown *T. fuciformis* to be beneficial to bone marrow regeneration, such as when bone marrow is damaged through cancer treatments. In addition, it is a potent source of Vitamin D, antioxidants, and fiber.

In one 2007 study published by the Cambridge University Press, polysaccharides derived from *T. fuciformis* were found to have a variety of benefits. These include stimulating the growth of immune organs such as the spleen and thymus, increasing the number and activities of many different cell types, and enhancing T-cell immune response. These effects have potential benefits in humans, but the study also outlined the possible uses in farming and livestock. The bioactive components of *T. fuciformis* and other mushrooms are hypothesized to improve productive performance and immune responses in chickens.

Tricholoma matsutake

Tricholoma matsutake, commonly referred to as matsutake, are a mycorrhizal mushroom that grows across North America (especially on the Washington state coast), Europe, and Asia. The "mycorrhizal" designation means a mushroom is closely associated with a specific plant. In the case of *T. matsutake*, the fungus has a symbiotic relationship with pine trees and is sometimes called the "pine mushroom". The mushroom is usually found at the base of pine trees, as the mycelium makes its home in the roots of the tree. Deforestation in different parts of the world has caused this species of fungus to be designated as "threatened" by the International Union for Conservation of Nature.

Matsutake mushrooms are usually a mix of white with brown spots. The firm, tall stem supports a cap of two to eight inches across. The spores are white and require a dark background to take a spore print. In the U.S., they are mostly found in Northern California and the Pacific Northwest. *T. matsutake* usually fruits in the fall and inspires a wave of mushroom hunters to search for them, similar to the morel mushroom craze of springtime. Due to the mycorrhizal nature of the mushroom, it has yet to be cultivated on a large scale. The symbiotic relationship between fungus and tree is difficult to replicate in a controlled environment.

The mushroom is especially popular in Japan, where premium varieties can fetch high prices. Much of the U.S. production of matsutake is exported to Japan because of the high demand in that country. They have a strong flavor that is often described as spicy or intense and most people either love them or hate them. When cooking with matsutake, the old adage "less is more" should be taken into consideration. The strong flavors can overwhelm a dish and might scare off your dinner guests that have not been acquainted with the mushroom. Younger mushrooms harvested in Japan are believed to be of higher quality and better flavor than older, imported varieties: the prized specimens can fetch over ten times the price of standard matsutake in Japan.

Matsutake has a history of human use dating back thousands of years. According to the Japan Special Forest Production Promotion Association, clay statues shaped like mushrooms, with one claimed to depict matsutake, were found in ruins from the Jomon Period that ranged from 14,000-1,000 BCE.

Recent studies have attempted to isolate the beneficial compounds found in *T. matsutake*. One such study found that polysaccharides present in the fungus exhibit anti-tumor, immuno-stimulation, anti-oxidation, and other biological activities. When the isolated compound was given to lab mice with tumors, the tumors dramatically reduced in size compared to a control group. In addition, the appetite, activity, and fur of the mice increased in quality as they were given the mushroom-derived compound.

In the same study, the polysaccharides from *T. matsutake* were also found to have strong antibacterial properties, fighting off a range of bacteria including *E. coli* and *Micrococcus lysodeikticus*.

Wolfporia cocos

Wolfiporia cocos, also known as hoelen, fuling, or tuckahoe, is a saprobic fungus found at the base of pine trees. The fungus produces a "sclerotium", which is a hard body that stores energy and keeps the individual alive under harsh conditions. This sclerotium is the part of the fungus that is usually harvested and used medicinally. The skin of the sclerotium is black and removed before use. The inside flesh is white and is referred to as "baifuling" in Chinese medicine. The fungus is commonly used and can be found in many Chinese herb shops and natural food stores.

W. cocos is of economic importance in Nigeria, as they use it for both food and medicine. In the U.S., Native Americans used the fungus to create a type of bread that settlers from Europe called "Indian bread". Tuckahoes are dug up in a similar fashion to potatoes and can weigh over a dozen pounds. The sclerotium can be ground up to produce flour that can then be baked into "Indian bread".

Traditional Chinese medicine has used *W. cocos* in a variety of ways, such as to clear dampness, balance the "stomach", and provide benefits to the "spleen". Additionally, it is used to sedate people, as a diuretic, to lower blood sugar, and to strengthen *qi*. In China, the fungus has also been used to treat jaundice and to bring on menstruation. In Korea, it is also used to induce menstruation, while also finding use as an antifertility treatment.

In lab studies with rats, an extract of *W. cocos* has been applied topically to the rats to successfully bring about hair growth. In another study, rats were purposefully given an autoimmune and inflammatory disease, encephalomyelitis. An extract from *W. cocos* successfully decreased the intensity of the disorder.

Acquiring Medicinal Mushrooms

Foraging

Gathering one's own mushrooms can be an enlightening activity. An adventure into the woods provides clean air, exercise, and the possibility of medicinal mushrooms, all of which are essential to our health and spirit. Many species of fungi featured in this book can be found worldwide and may even be near your home, including *Trametes versicolor, Ganoderma lucidum*, and others. Gathering wild mushrooms can be an entirely sustainable source of food, medicine, and amusement, as long as certain guidelines are followed.

- When harvesting a mushroom with a stalk, slice the base with a knife or carefully twist and pull them out. Be sure not to disturb the mycelium living below the surface to ensure its future viability and production.

- When gathering conks (stemless mushrooms protruding from trees), always leave a few behind to allow spore distribution to continue. As a perennial fungus, the species will rely on these conks to release spores to inhabit other trees in the forest.

- A general guideline to follow when engaging in any outdoor activity is to "Leave No Trace". Walk lightly so nobody can tell that you visited the area and be sure to cover any holes left from picked mushrooms with leaves or dirt.

An obvious worry when collecting wild mushrooms for consumption is the possibility of picking a poisonous one. Acknowledging this possibility is healthy, and while poisonous mushrooms are a reality, most mushrooms are not harmful. Before foraging with the intent to pick and consume, head out on the trails with a mushroom guidebook and learn to properly identify your local species.

Education and experience will be your greatest allies in ensuring you correctly identify mushroom species. If you are ever in doubt, consult a professional.

Many colleges and mycology clubs offer weekend seminars and educational opportunities for beginning mushroom hunters. These groups and events can be an invaluable source of knowledge, especially for species and hunting techniques for your local area.

Buying Fresh

If you are lucky enough to live next to a natural food store or a Chinese market, you probably have fresh mushrooms available to you for many parts of the year. Even if not, many supermarkets are getting on the bandwagon and making fresh mushrooms available to their customers. Farmer's markets are an excellent source of mushrooms, as you are usually able to speak to the mushroom cultivator in person and find out their growing techniques and quality. If you can source fresh specimens, there are a few things to keep in mind when purchasing.

Fresh mushrooms have less room for contamination and misinformation that is common in the supplement industry. However, always be sure to check for any moldy spots caused by improper packaging. Cut off the infected portion or discard the mushroom in its entirety. Also, "organic" mushrooms are usually indicative of high-quality mushrooms, but growing practices and pesticide usage also needs to be investigated and considered.

Buying Dried or Prepared

Sometimes, reading the nutrition label isn't enough to determine the efficacy of a medicinal mushroom product. The potency of a product is determined by a few different things, such as extraction method, part of the mushroom used, and other factors.

First of all, look for dual extracted products. Most products will detail their method of extraction. Dual extraction collects all bioactive compounds from a mushroom, while a single extraction will only collect either the fat soluble or water-soluble compounds. Companies that go through the time to do a dual extraction are more likely a trustworthy source of medicine.

When possible, purchase the fruiting body of a species, rather than an extract or powder. The fruiting bodies tend to have the highest amount of nutrients and active healing compounds. They are the part of fungi that humans have consumed for thousands of years. Today, many cultivators will take extracts of the mycelium culture, which may also include extracted compounds from the substrate used to grow the mycelium. This saves the producers time by not having to fruit their cultures, but the products end up being unsatisfactory when compared to real, mushroom-derived products. While there are health benefits in the mycelium of many species, only purchase these products if that is what you are specifically looking for. If you are seeking a certain mushroom/fruiting body, buy the real thing.

If possible, investigate the growing practices of the mushroom cultivator. Organically grown mushrooms are a good start, while mushrooms grown without pesticides and other harmful agricultural products are best.

Not all mushrooms are grown the same. Different specimens of the same species can have different levels of the important bioactive compounds that you are seeking to ingest. Rather than purchasing based on weight alone, you are often able to purchase mushrooms products based on the level of polysaccharides or glucans found in the product. This is a better way to measure your doses and ensures that the product has been through lab testing. A good baseline is that mushroom extracts should be composed of at least 20% polysaccharides, one of the most heavily researched and health-benefiting compounds found in medicinal mushrooms.

Growing Your Own

Growing your own is a sustainable and low-cost way of creating your own supply of medicinal mushrooms. It just takes a little time and dedication. The simplest way to get started is to start an outdoor mushroom patch.

Finding a suitable site for your outdoor mushroom patch should be simple; just choose a place that you have seen mushrooms flourish in the past! A gentle slope (to avoid water buildup) and shrubs or bushes (to shade from the sun) are good locations to look out for. A good location can be a garden bed that you already have established, as the mushrooms will not compete with your plants and will provide nutrients as they decompose organic matter. Otherwise, preparing a large bed of wood chips or sawdust will work for many different species.

Ensure that your mushroom patch will have adequate access to moisture, either naturally or through regular watering. Always choose a shady location over a sunny one. Similarly, north facing slopes usually work better than south facing slopes. All this being said, feel free to experiment and try different locations for different species, depending on their exact needs.

Once your site is chosen and prepared, you can inoculate your beds with sawdust or grain spawn. "Spawn" refers to a culture of mycelium that has established itself in a medium of wood or grain. This spawn can be broken up and spread into your outdoor mushroom beds, where the mycelium will continue to spread and take residence. Several species of spawn are readily available for purchase, such as *G. frondosa, P. ostreatus, and L. edodes*. While it is entirely possible to grow mushrooms from spores or other methods, commercial spawn is the easiest and quickest method to get your backyard bed producing mushrooms.

Before applying your spawn, moisten the beds thoroughly. Mycelium craves moisture, especially early in its growth. Paul Stamets, a popular mycologist, recommends that your bed should be around 20% spawn and 80% substrate. This ratio ensures a fast rate of growth without wasting your spawn. When using less spawn, there is a higher possibility of other, less-desirable mushrooms taking over part of your mushroom bed. Colonization time can take anywhere from 1 to 8 weeks.

You may inoculate the beds anytime from early spring until early fall. You should avoid inoculation too late into the winter, as the cold temperatures will prevent the mycelium from growing. However, if given enough time to establish, most species can survive the winter due to the heat produced and retained by underground decomposition.

Once the mycelium is established, you have the option to attempt to fruit your bed or to expand the mycelium even further. If you wish to expand, just spread another thin layer of substrate across the top of your established bed. The mycelium will immediately begin to colonize the new material.

At some point, you will want to fruit your beds and collect your edible mushrooms! To trigger fruiting, you must simulate fall weather by providing frequent shade, as most species produce mushrooms in the fall. Frequent watering is also encouraged. Make sure to induce fruiting after the mycelium have fully colonized your substrate, as the rate of colonization dramatically decreases as the mycelium focuses on mushroom production.

Storing Fresh Mushrooms

When storing fresh, fleshy mushrooms such as oyster or shiitake, it is recommended to dry them. Food dehydrators are affordable and make a great investment if you are serious about food preservation - mushrooms or otherwise. Dried mushrooms stored in an airtight jar can easily have a shelf life of six or more months, depending on the species.

Larger "conk" mushrooms, such as *Ganoderma lucidum*, will dry on their own and maintain the same appearance and medicinal properties for years. They can even be kept as an ornament or house décor, ready to be used medicinally at any time.

Incorporating Mushrooms Into Your Diet

General Tips and Preparation

The simplest way to incorporate the nutrients and benefits of mushrooms is to eat them fresh! Always make sure to cook mushrooms before eating, as many contain a toxic substance (hydrazine) that are neutralized when cooking. You can bake, boil, fry, or grill mushrooms, as well as preparing them into teas and tinctures. Dried mushrooms can be rehydrated and used in similar ways to fresh mushrooms. We have provided recipes below to get your ideas flowing, so feel free to experiment with and find your own mushroom-cooking inspiration! And again, it is not recommended to consume fresh, raw mushrooms due to the toxins found within. Cook them first!

If the mushroom can't be eaten fresh due to texture or toughness, it can usually be dried and ground into a powder. This is especially true of most polypore fungi, such as *Ganoderma lucidum* (reishi) or *Inonotus obliquus* (chaga). The resulting powder can be added to soups, gravies, or any meal to add flavor and medicinal benefits. Adding mushroom powder to a smoothie or protein shake is a quick and easy way to incorporate them into your diet. The powder could also be added to your morning coffee for a positive start to your day.

If you aren't often in the kitchen, mushroom supplement capsules are another popular way to add mushrooms to your diet. Mushroom capsules are a common commercial preparation, or you can even prepare the capsules yourself from dried mushrooms. Always be careful when purchasing commercial medicinal mushroom products, as misinformation and mislabeling is common in the industry.

Medicinal Preparations

Hot Water Extraction

Hot water extraction is another term for "mushroom tea". In this method, hot water is used to extract any water-soluble compounds found in a medicinal mushroom. This method is popular and effective because the main active ingredients in most mushrooms, beta-glucans and polysaccharides, are water-soluble. Beta-glucans and polysaccharides are responsible for many of the medicinal properties of mushrooms, including anti-tumor, anti-inflammatory, and immune boosting properties.

To perform a hot water extraction, you will first want to process your mushrooms. If using fresh, cut the mushrooms into small slices. Dried mushrooms can easily be broken down into smaller pieces. Next, fill a pot with 2 cups of water and bring to a boil. Add 2 oz. of mushroom material to the liquid. Simmer the mixture for up to 3 hours. Longer simmering times will lead to fully extracted mushrooms and concentrated liquid. Allow the mixture to cool and strain out the mushroom material. The spent material can be saved and used again for a future extraction.

Enjoy the tea fresh or save in an airtight glass jar and store in the fridge.

The measurements of water and mushroom material can be adjusted depending on the potency and dosage you are looking for.

Tincture

Producing a tincture is a tried and true method of preserving the active ingredients inside mushrooms and herbs. A tincture collects the fat-soluble compounds from a mushroom, while a dual extraction goes one step further and gathers the water-soluble compounds. While a tincture provides most of the benefits of a mushroom species, a dual extraction is usually considered a more complete and fully potent extraction method.

To perform the tincture extraction, you will need 190 proof clear grain alcohol diluted 1:1 with distilled water. If that is not available to you, 80-100 proof vodka makes a fine substitute. The rest of the process is rather simple. First, chop up your dried mushrooms and place them into a blender. Add just enough grain alcohol to cover the mushrooms. Blend the two together until the mixture is smooth and consistent. Pour the mixture into a Mason jar of appropriate size. After about 30 minutes, the mixture should separate with the mushroom mass floating to the bottom. There should be approximately one inch of an alcohol layer on top to prevent any fermentation from occurring. Cover the jar and keep it somewhere out of direct sunlight. Give the jar a good shake every day.

After about two weeks, the medicinal properties of the mushrooms should be well-extracted. You can strain the mushrooms out of the liquid, squeezing the excess moisture out to retain as much of the medicine as possible. If you store the mostly clear liquid in a glass jar, it should retain its benefits for around two to three years. This method is considered a single extraction and should contain most of the active compounds and medicinal properties.

Dual Extraction

If you are looking for a more complete extraction, you can go a step further after the tincture and perform a double extraction. To perform this extra step, you will need the used mushroom mash from the tincture extraction, also called the "marc". Add the marc to a pot with five times its volume of water. For example, one cup of marc would require five cups of water. Simmer on low for one hour. Let the concoction cool before squeezing out the moisture from the marc and discarding it.

Next, you will want to simmer the remaining liquid on low heat, until around 80% of the liquid has evaporated. Add this concentrated liquid to your original tincture from the single extraction method. Make sure to keep the alcohol content of your tincture above 20% to ensure that no fermentation or unwanted growth will occur. This double extraction should provide the full medicinal benefits from most mushrooms, similar to the effects if eaten whole. Tincture can be enjoyed daily by adding a dose to your tea or a glass of water. Be sure to follow any recommended dosing guidelines for your specific mushroom species.

Dosing

It is recommended to take tonics like medicinal mushrooms and herbs in courses. Depending on the mushroom, you will want to take them for at least three months and no longer than a year at a time. This ensures that the benefits will take effect, while giving yourself a break period will allow your body to flush out any buildups of unneeded compounds. Be sure to follow any recommended dosing guidelines for your specific mushroom species and product, as the concentrations and potency can vary wildly.

Recipes

The best way to share mushrooms with others is through a delicious meal or beverage. We have provided a large variety of recipes here that cover everything from Asian stir-frys and soups to Indian, Mexican, and Italian cuisines. There should be something for everyone. Nobody should have an excuse not to add a bit of mushrooms to their diet!

Reishi Tea

Reishi tea is the quintessential medicinal mushroom recipe. Reishi mushrooms are one of the most popular and widely researched fungi, leading to heavy marketing and use in the health food industry. It makes a great substitute for coffee in the morning, providing a wellness boost without the negative effects often associated with coffee.

Ingredients:

- 1 oz. whole dried reishi mushrooms

Instructions:

1. Finely chop the mushrooms and grind into a powder, using a spice mill or a mortar and pestle. If you are unable to source fresh mushrooms, reishi can often be purchased in pre-ground form.

2. Wrap the powder in muslin or a tea bag of your choice.

3. Bring two cups of water to a boil. Drop the bag of powdered reishi into the water. Simmer until the liquid has been reduced by half, or about 1 hour.

4. Enjoy. It is not advised to drink more than one cup daily. Also, limit your intake to no more than a month at a time to avoid any possible side effects from long term consumption.

5. Excess tea can be refrigerated for approximately five days.

Chaga Tea

Chaga, like reishi, is one of those legendary medicinal mushrooms that enjoys frequent and dedicated use by a large amount of people. Also, like reishi, chaga tea makes a great alternative to your morning coffee. Its benefits have been tested and reported by folk medicine practitioners around the world.

Ingredients:

- 1 oz. whole dried chaga mushrooms
- honey (optional)

Instructions:

1. Finely chop the mushrooms and grind into a powder, using a spice mill or a mortar and pestle. If you are unable to source fresh mushrooms, chaga can often be purchased in pre-ground form.

2. Wrap the powder in muslin or a tea bag of your choice.

3. Bring two cups of water to a boil. Drop the bag of powdered chaga into the water. Simmer until the liquid has been reduced by half, or about 1 hour.

4. Enjoy. Feel free to add a splash of honey or other sweetener if you require.

5. Excess tea can be refrigerated for approximately five days.

Chaga Anti-Inflammatory Smoothie

Any smoothie or protein shake can benefit from the addition of medicinal mushrooms. This anti-inflammatory smoothie features chaga (Inonotus obliquus), but feel free to use a mushroom (usually in powder or tea form) that fits your needs.

Ingredients:

- 1 medium sized banana, ripe
- 1.5 cups nut milk of your choice
- 1/2 cup chaga mushroom tea, cooled
- 2 tablespoons almond butter or nut butter of choice
- 2 tablespoons hemp hearts
- 1 pinch fresh turmeric
- 1 pinch fresh ginger
- 1 pinch cardamom
- 1 pinch black pepper
- 1 tablespoon raw cacao powder
- 1-2 medium sized medjool dates pitted
- 1 teaspoon maple syrup
- 1/4 teaspoon cinnamon
- 1-2 cups crushed ice

You can substitute fresh ingredients for dried, such as with turmeric and ginger, if you require.

Instructions:

1. Add all main ingredients to a blender. Blend on high until consistency is smooth.

2. Serve in a glass or to-go cup and enjoy!

To get the most nutritional impact/benefit, enjoy immediately after preparing.

Golden Mushroom Milk

This drink entices you with its gorgeous color, but it will keep you wanting more with its wellness-boosting benefits. Turmeric is commonly used for its anti-inflammatory properties and makes a great sidekick to reishi mushrooms. Enjoy!

Ingredients:

- 1 tsp. ghee (or substitute coconut oil)
- 1 tsp. reishi mushroom powder
- 1 tsp. turmeric
- ¼ tsp. freshly grated ginger
- ¼ tsp. cinnamon powder
- ¼ tsp. freshly ground black pepper
- 2 cups almond milk (or milk of your choice)
- 2 tsp. honey

Instructions:

1. Heat coconut oil or ghee on medium heat in a small soup pot.

2. Add turmeric, ginger, cinnamon and black pepper. Let cook for about 1 minute.

3. Add the milk and honey. Bring to a boil and whisk well.

4. Serve and enjoy!

Mushroom Butter Coffee

Butter or "bulletproof" coffee is considered a fad by many and a health-boosting, daily ritual by others. Either way, it is a tasty way to consume your cup of morning joe, so adding a dose of medicinal mushrooms will only make the beverage more beneficial. It is often used for people on a ketogenic diet, as the fat from the butter and coconut oil help suppress hunger and sustain the body until lunch. The drink is definitely worth a try, but do your own research before making it a part of your daily routine.

Ingredients:
- 1 cup of hot, freshly brewed coffee
- 1/2 tablespoon ghee OR unsalted grass-fed butter
- 1/2 tablespoon coconut oil
- 1 dose of a mushroom tincture of your choice

Instructions:
1. Combine the fresh coffee, ghee or butter, coconut oil, and mushroom tincture in a blender.

2. Blend on high for about 20 seconds. Be cautious when opening the blender, as the steam from the coffee will likely be very hot.

3. Serve immediately and enjoy. For a more luxurious experience, feel free to add cacao powder, vanilla extract, cinnamon, or another addition of your choice.

Mushroom Cold Brew Iced Tea

By now, you probably realize that mushroom tinctures can be added to just about any beverage to give it a dose of medicinal power. So, we will give you just this one last beverage recipe for inspiration, after which you can get creative and add the tincture to any of your favorite drinks. This mushroom cold brew iced tea is refreshing and won't have the astringent, tannic taste found in regular hot tea.

Ingredients:
- 1 bag of tea, or 1 teaspoon loose-leaf tea per 8 ounces of water (green is recommended, but any tea will do)
- 1 dose of mushroom tincture per 8 ounces of water
- fresh mint leaves
- sliced cucumber
- sliced lemon

Instructions:
1. Put your tea bags or loose-leaf tea into a glass pitcher. Pour in cool, filtered water.

2. Keep the pitcher covered and refrigerate. Depending on the type of tea and the concentration desired, steep for about 6-10 hours

3. After steeping, remove the tea bags or strain the loose-leaf tea using a fine mesh sieve. Discard the tea leaves.

4. Add the mushroom tincture, lemon slices, mint leaves, and cucumber slices and allow to soak for another hour.

5. Serve and enjoy! Leave the lemon, mint leaves, and cucumber in the jar to continue to add flavor. Enjoy within 3-5 days.

Medicinal Mushroom Broth

This sipping broth, like most bone broth recipes, is for a chilly morning or cozy afternoon for a boost of immunity. Plus, it is super easy to make. Mushrooms like reishi, chaga, and shiitake are powerful allies to add to your kitchen staples!

You will need some garlic, onions, and fresh herbs of your choice like sage, rosemary, or fennel to add a boost of flavor to your broth. This nourishing broth is savory and vibrant, featuring all of the benefits of medicinal mushrooms.

Ingredients:

- 10 dried shiitake mushrooms
- 10 slices dried reishi mushroom
- ½ cup dried chaga mushroom
- 2 pounds chicken bones
- 1 large onion
- 3 bulbs garlic
- 5 celery stalks
- 2 tablespoons extra virgin olive oil
- 1 cup white wine

- 4 quarts water
- fresh herbs (optional)

Instructions:

1. Heat oven to 300 degrees Fahrenheit. Line a baking sheet or pan with parchment paper. Arrange bones, garlic, onion, celery, and medicinal mushrooms on the sheet. Drizzle with extra virgin olive oil. Slow roast the components together for about 45 minutes for maximum fragrance.

2. Transfer the contents on the baking sheet into a stock pot. Then, pour in the wine and water. Bring to a boil over medium-high heat. Then turn down temp to medium-low and simmer uncovered for 6-8 hours. Stir in fresh herbs for about 15 minutes before removing from heat.

3. Turn off the heat. Strain the broth and discard the leftover components. Serve hot immediately, or store in the fridge for up to 5 days. You may store in the freezer for up to 3 months. Adjust seasoning with fine sea salt before serving your Medicinal Mushroom Broth.

How to Use

- use as a base for a delicious soup or stew
- sip on it when you need a little extra nourishment
- cook your grains in it

This Medicinal Mushroom Broth is a beneficial broth to bring out when you need a little extra boost of immune support. Nourish yourself with a cup of hot broth made with fresh herbs and mushrooms with this simple recipe.

Shiitake Stir Fry

Stir fry is a quick and easy way to incorporate mushrooms into your meal. Follow this easy recipe for a delicious shiitake mushroom stir fry that includes many vegetables and unique flavors.

Ingredients:

- 1 tbsp toasted sesame oil
- 1½ cups whole shiitake mushrooms (dried is fine too)
- 1 red pepper, seeded and chopped
- 1 tsp chopped ginger
- ½ tsp chopped garlic
- ¼ tsp red pepper flakes
- 2 carrots, cut into matchstick shapes
- 1 cups sugar snap peas
- 1 cup bean sprouts
- 4 scallions, sliced thinly
- 1 tsp brown sugar
- 1½ tsp soy sauce
- 1 cup low-sodium vegetable broth
- 1 cup cooked brown rice

Instructions:

1. In a large skillet or wok, heat sesame oil over medium-high heat.

2. Add shiitake mushrooms, red bell pepper, ginger, garlic, and red pepper flakes, stirring constantly. Continue to cook for about 5 minutes.

3. Add the carrots, snap peas, bean sprouts, and scallions to the skillet. Stir-fry for about 2 minutes.

4. In a small bowl, dissolve brown sugar in soy sauce. Add the mixture to the pan.

5. Pour in the vegetable broth; cook for about 2 minutes, until the mixture comes to a boil and starts to thicken. Serve over brown rice.

Nabemono

In Japan, a Chanko Nabemono (Sumo Stew) is a hot pot filled with plenty of vegetables and protein sources like chicken, shrimp, and tofu. You can even use this to try out the maitake mushroom in quite a unique dish. This dish is traditionally eaten by sumo wrestlers, but can be easily enjoyed at home by anyone.

Ingredients:

Stew

- 1 ½ lb cod fillet
- 8 shrimp
- 6 oz sliced pork belly
- 4 boneless, skinless chicken thighs
- 1 package medium-firm tofu (approximately 14 oz)
- ½ head napa cabbage
- 6 green onions/scallions
- 4-6 maitake mushrooms
- ¼ carrot

Broth

- 6 cups chicken broth
- ¼ cup sake
- ⅓ cup mirin
- 2 tbsp ginger juice (use grater)
- 1 ½ tsp crushed garlic
- ½ cup miso (preferably white miso)

For Serving

- sesame sauce
- 4-6 cups udon noodles

Instructions:

How to Make the Broth

1. Gather all of your broth ingredients. Over medium heat, combine the broth, sake, ginger juice, mirin, garlic, in a stock pot. Bring to a simmer.

2. In a small bowl add the miso, and several spoons full of broth. Mix together until smooth.

3. Then gradually add the miso mixture to the broth in the pot. Whisking to avoid clumps. Once the miso has been added, do not let the broth boil.

How to Cook the Dish: Sumo Stew

When cooking the stew ingredients (see Ingredients) on the stove top, cook in batches.

1. Add a small amount of each of the ingredients to the broth, simmer (do not boil) until cooked, and serve them, returning to the stove to start a new batch as each previous batch is eaten. The vegetables and tofu cook more quickly than meat, seafood, and chicken.

2. Keep the broth at a simmer the entire time. If the liquid gets low, add a little water or chicken broth to have enough liquid to heat the noodles at the end.

3. Remove any solids in the broth and add the noodles. Simmer until heated through, then ladle into the soup bowls and serve.

Maitake mushrooms are a great addition to this recipe or feel free to substitute any other edible mushroom, such as shiitake. Enjoy the benefits of these medicinal mushrooms in a delicious, traditional Japanese dish.

Mushroom Stroganoff

You heard that right. This cozy classic comfort food becomes even more delicious when it is packed with powerful medicinal mushrooms. You can use just about any of your favorite mushrooms for this recipe.

Ingredients:

- 1 pound wide egg noodles
- 3 tbsp butter, divided
- 1 small white onion, thinly sliced
- 4 cloves garlic, minced
- 1 pound baby bella mushrooms*
- 1/2 cup dry white wine
- 1.5 cups vegetable stock
- 1 tablespoon Worcestershire sauce (here is a vegetarian brand)
- 3 1/2 tablespoons flour
- 3 small sprigs of fresh thyme (or 1/4 teaspoon dried thyme)
- 1/2 cup plain Greek yogurt or light sour cream
- kosher salt
- black pepper
- optional toppings: freshly-grated Parmesan cheese, chopped fresh parsley, extra black pepper.

Instructions:

1. Cook egg noodles al dente in boiling, generously-salted water according to package instructions.

2. Melt 1 tablespoon butter in a large saucepan over medium-high heat. Add onions and sauté for 5 minutes, stirring occasionally.

3. Add the remaining 2 tablespoons butter, garlic and mushrooms, and stir to combine. Continue sautéing for an additional 5-7 minutes, until the mushrooms are cooked and tender.

4. Add the white wine, and deglaze the pan by using a wooden spoon to scrape the brown bits off the bottom of the pan. Let the sauce simmer for 3 minutes.

5. Meanwhile, in a separate bowl, whisk together the vegetable stock, Worcestershire and flour until smooth. Pour the vegetable stock mixture into the pan, along with the thyme. Stir to combine.

6. Let the mixture simmer for an additional 5 minutes, stirring occasionally, until it starts to thicken. Then, stir in the Greek yogurt (or sour cream) evenly into the sauce. Taste, and season with a pinch of two of salt and pepper as needed.

7. Serve immediately over the egg noodles, garnished with any toppings you desire.

Creamy Mushroom Soup

This creamy mushroom soup recipe can be made with all different kinds of mushrooms, depending on your preference.

Ingredients:

- ¼ cup of unsalted butter
- 2 pounds sliced fresh mushrooms (cremini, shiitake, or oyster are recommended)
- 1 pinch salt
- 1 yellow onion, diced
- 1 ½ tablespoons all-purpose flour
- 6 sprigs fresh thyme
- 2 cloves garlic, peeled
- 4 cups chicken broth

- 1 cup water
- 1 cup heavy whipping cream
- 1 pinch salt and freshly ground black pepper to taste
- 1 teaspoon fresh thyme leaves for garnish

Instructions:

1. Melt butter in a large soup pot over medium-high heat; cook mushrooms in butter with 1 pinch salt until the mushrooms give off their juices; reduce heat to low. Continue to cook, stirring often, until juices evaporate and the mushrooms are golden brown, or about 15 minutes. Set aside a few attractive mushroom slices for garnish later, if desired. Mix onion into mushrooms and cook until onion is soft and translucent, about 5 more minutes.

2. Stir flour into mushroom mixture and cook, stirring often, for 2 minutes to remove raw flour taste. Tie thyme sprigs into a small bundle with kitchen twine and add to mushroom mixture; add garlic cloves. Pour chicken stock and water into mushroom mixture. Bring to a simmer and cook for 1 hour. Remove thyme bundle.

3. Transfer soup to a blender in small batches and puree on high speed until smooth and thick.

4. Return soup to pot and stir in cream. Season with salt and black pepper and serve in bowls, garnished with reserved mushroom slices and a few thyme leaves.

Porcini Risotto

Porcini risotto is a fall favorite in Italy, where the mushrooms from *B. edulis* are especially popular. Feel free to substitute for a different mushroom if you don't have porcinis on hand.

Ingredients:

- 1 ounces dried porcini mushrooms

- 3 cups chicken stock
- ¼ cup extra-virgin olive oil
- 1 small shallot, minced
- 1 garlic clove, minced
- 1 cup arborio rice
- ¼ cup dry white wine
- 1 small bay leaf
- 1 tablespoon unsalted butter
- 1 tablespoon mascarpone
- 1 cup parmesan cheese
- 1 pound fresh porcini, thinly sliced
- 1 thyme sprig
- Salt and ground pepper

Instructions:

1. Boil 2 ½ cups of water. Soak the dried porcini mushrooms in this boiling water, using a heatproof bowl. Soak for approximately 10 minutes or until softened. Drain the mushrooms, keeping 1 cup of the soaking water. Rinse the mushrooms clean of any dirt. Finely chop the mushrooms and set them aside. Pour the previously reserved soaking water into a saucepan, being sure not to stop before the sediment is poured. Stir the chicken stock into the saucepan and season to taste with salt and pepper. Warm the stock on low heat.

2. Heat two tablespoons of olive oil in a large saucepan. Add the garlic and shallots, stirring over medium heat until softened, or around 2 minutes. Add the rehydrated porcini and arborio rice, stirring to mix the contents evenly. Add the white wine and a bay leaf, cooking until the wine has evaporated.

3. Add about 25% of the stock from step 1 and cook over medium heat, stirring constantly. The stock should be nearly absorbed by the rice. Repeat this step, adding the stock in batches and constantly stirring. After about 20 minutes, the rice should be al dente and floating in a creamy sauce. Discard the bay leaf. Stir in the butter, cheese, and mascarpone. Season with salt and pepper to taste and keep warm.

4. In a frying pan, heat 2 tablespoons of oil. Add the fresh porcini (or substitute mushrooms of your choice) and thyme and cook over high heat. Stir often and cook until softened and golden, or around 8 minutes. Remove and discard the thyme. Season the mushrooms to taste with salt and pepper. Display the fried mushrooms over the risotto and serve.

Lion's Mane Burgers

Vegetarian burgers, anyone? With the buttery, fish-like flavor of lion's mane mushrooms, these burgers will be something special.

Ingredients:

- 4 ciabatta rolls, or other bun of your choice
- 1 medium Lion's Mane mushroom
- 4 slices of Swiss cheese
- 1 white onion
- 4 tbsp butter
- 1 tbsp extra virgin olive oil
- Salt and ground pepper

Instructions:

1. Slice the onion into thin strips. Saute the onion slices in a pan with 1 tbsp of olive oil and 1 tbsp of butter on medium

heat. Remove from heat when they have caramelized to your liking, or about 5-10 minutes.

2. Slice the mushroom into steaks around 1/2 inch thick, or around 4-6 ounces each. Slice in a way that they are the most "circular" or burger-shaped that they can be. Place the mushrooms in a non-stick skillet and cook over medium heat.

3. Cook the mushrooms for 3-5 minutes and flip when browned, adding salt and pepper to taste on each side. Once they are almost browned, add one tbsp of butter to the pan, ensuring that both sides of all mushrooms are coated. Cook until golden and fried, or around 2 minutes on each side. Remove from the pan.

4. Toast the rolls or buns in the same pan, adding up to 1 tbsp of butter for a golden brown crisp. Place a slice of swiss cheese on each roll, covering the pan so as to melt the cheese.

5. Add a lion's mane steak and grilled onions to each roll.

6. Serve and enjoy!

Alfredo Mushroom Pasta

A "shroomy" take on the classic chicken alfredo dish. Because of the indulgent nature of this dish, it's an easy way to introduce mushrooms to picky eaters.

Ingredients:

- 2 tablespoons olive oil
- ¾ pound fresh oyster mushrooms, sliced
- ¼ pound fresh shiitake mushrooms, stemmed and sliced
- 2 cloves garlic, minced
- 2 fluid ounces dry white wine
- 1 cup chicken stock
- 1 cup heavy whipping cream
- 8 ounces fettuccine pasta
- 1 ½ teaspoons chopped fresh thyme
- 1 ½ teaspoons chopped fresh chives
- 1 ½ teaspoons chopped fresh Italian parsley
- 9 tablespoons freshly shredded parmesan cheese
- salt and ground black pepper

Instructions:

1. In a large skillet, heat olive oil over medium heat. Add in the oyster and shiitake mushrooms with a pinch of salt to the hot oil. Cook until the mushroom juice evaporates and the mushrooms have browned, but not burned. Around 8-10 minutes.

2. Add garlic to the skillet and cook for 1 minute; pour in the white wine and cook until it nearly evaporates. Add the chicken stock into the mushroom skillet, seasoning with salt and black pepper to taste. Lower the heat to a simmer and cook until the sauce thickens, or around 5 minutes.

3. Add cream to the skillet, stirring frequently while cooking for about 5 minutes. The mixture should foam and thicken even further.

4. Fill a large stock pot with water and a pinch of salt. Bring to a boil. Stir in the fettuccine pasta, bringing the water back to a boil before reducing to a simmer on medium heat. Cook pasta until al dente, or about 8 minutes. Drain the pasta but do not rinse it. Store in a heat proof bowl and keep warm.

5. Stir the herbs (thyme, chives, and Italian parsley) into the mushroom sauce and turn off the heat; mix in 1/2 cup of parmesan cheese and stir until the cheese is melted and combined.

6. Add a portion of pasta to each serving plate. Add sauce, reserving the mushrooms in the pan. Toss the pasta in the sauce before adding the mushrooms on top. Garnish with herbs and remaining parmesan cheese. Serve and enjoy!

Mushroom and Avocado Sushi

Mushrooms replace the fish in this vegetarian take on sushi. This mushroom and avocado sushi is a great recipe to make with a friend - rolling sushi is a fun skill to learn!

Ingredients:

- 4 ounces fresh shiitake mushrooms
- 2 tbsp soy sauce
- 1 tbsp sesame oil + extra for frying

- 4 big sheets seaweed
- 1 cup sushi rice
- 1 avocado sliced
- 1 cucumber halved lengthwise, then quartered lengthwise
- 4 green onions cut to be slightly longer than the seaweed
- 1/4 cup pickled ginger

Instructions:

1. Start cooking the rice.

2. In a medium skillet, heat a few drops of sesame oil over medium high heat. Add the shiitake mushrooms and sauté for 4-7 minutes, or until golden and fragrant. Add the soy sauce, tossing the mushrooms, and cook until darkened. Pull off the heat and mix in the 1 tbsp of sesame oil.

3. Place a bamboo sushi rolling mat on a cutting board, and drape a piece of plastic wrap big enough to cover the mat on top. Fill a small bowl with water and keep handy.

4. Place a sheet of seaweed on the rolling mat. Add about 1/4 cup rice, keeping the top and bottom edges free of rice. Use your fingers to break up and spread the rice.

5. Place two rows of mushrooms in the middle of the rice, stretching from the left to the right edge. Press them into the rice gently to help them stick. Place a few avocado slices across the rice. Add 2 pieces of cucumber and 1 green

onion. Set pieces of pickled ginger across the other ingredients.

6. Starting from the bottom end, roll up the sushi tightly using the bamboo mat. Once you get a few inches away from the top edge, start to keep the bamboo mat out of the rolling process, and use the plastic wrap to guide the rest. Once the sushi is sealed, give it a few squeezes to make sure it's sticking together, then unwrap from the plastic wrap and sushi mat, and let cool seam side down.

7. Using a serrated knife, slice the sushi. Thicker slices are usually better. Serve at room temperature and enjoy!

Italian Mushroom Omelet

Omelets have long been the test of a competent chef. Luckily, you don't need to be an accomplished chef to follow this recipe! You might already have your own omelet recipe, but no mushroom recipe list would be complete without a mushroom omelet! Feel free to substitute the cremini mushrooms with a species that is available locally to you.

Ingredients:

- 2 tablespoons extra virgin olive oil
- 1 small onion, diced
- 2 oz. cremini mushrooms
- salt and ground black pepper
- 1 garlic clove, minced

- 2 teaspoons Italian parsley, finely chopped
- 3 eggs
- 1 tablespoon minced chives, finely chopped
- 2 teaspoons low-fat milk
- 1/2 oz. parmesan cheese, grated
- 1/2 oz. mozzarella cheese, grated

Instructions:

1. Trim off the ends of the mushrooms. Dice the mushrooms to approximately 1/2-inch width. Heat a skillet or frying pan to medium-high heat and add 1 tablespoon of extra virgin olive oil. Add your diced onions (approximately 2 tablespoons, or to taste) and cook until the onions begin to sweat, around 2 minutes. Add the diced mushrooms and cook, stirring or tossing frequently. When the mushrooms begin to soften, add your minced garlic clove and continue to cook for approximately 5 minutes, or until the mushrooms are cooked through and tender. Add salt and pepper to taste.

2. After adding the garlic to the pan in step 1, begin to prepare your eggs by cracking 3 eggs into a bowl. Add the milk and whisk vigorously with a fork until the yolks and whites have combined. After the mushrooms have cooked through (step 1), add 1 tablespoon of olive oil and pour in your egg mixture. Give the ingredients a quick stir to make sure the mushrooms are evenly distributed throughout the eggs. Cover the pan with a tight-fitting lid. The steam created from the tight-fitting lid will help cook through the eggs and provide a fluffy texture.

3. After a minute or two, tilt the pan and gently life the edges of the omelet with a spatula to allow the less-cooked eggs to run underneath. After another minute or two, and before the bottom becomes too browned, lift the pan and give it a quick flick away and then back towards yourself to flip the omelet (it's all in the wrist!).

4. Immediately add the parmesan and mozzarella cheese evenly across the now-cooked top of the omelet. Reapply the lid for another two to three minutes, or until cooked on the bottom. Carefully old the omelet in half and apply the Italian parsley and chives across the top. Gently slide the complete omelet onto a plate and serve.

Pepper and Mushroom Fajitas

As with all of our recipes, feel free to substitute for any mushrooms that are currently available in your area.

Ingredients:
Fajitas

- 1 pound oyster mushrooms, rinsed and pat dry
- 1 medium white onion
- 4 medium Anaheim peppers
- 8 to 10 corn tortillas
- ⅔ cup grated or crumbled cotija cheese
- 1 tablespoon extra-virgin olive oil

Marinade

- ¼ cup extra-virgin olive oil
- 2 limes, juiced

- 1 small habanero pepper, finely chopped
- ½ teaspoon ground cumin
- ½ teaspoon ground coriander
- ¼ teaspoon ground chile powder
- sea salt and black pepper

Avocado Sauce
- 2 large avocados
- ⅓ cup fresh cilantro
- 2 tablespoons fresh parsley
- ½ lime, juiced
- 2 tablespoons water
- sea salt and black pepper

Instructions:

1. Slice the mushrooms into strips with a width of approximately 1/2 inch, creating steak-like strips. Cut off the tops of the Anaheim peppers. Slice them in half and remove any seeds. Slice the peppers into strips with a width of approximately 1/2 inch, similar to the mushrooms. Keep the length of the peppers to 4 inches or less. Slice off both ends of the white onion. Place the onion on one of the flat sides and slice the onion in half, from top to bottom (rather than through the middle/side). Place one half of the onion on your cutting board and slice strips, approximately 1/4" thick. At this point, the onion slices should be half of a circle in shape. Toss the sliced oyster mushrooms, sliced Anaheim peppers, and sliced onions in a bowl.

2. In a small bowl, combine the marinade ingredients and whisk until well-combined. Add the marinade to the bowl of mixed vegetables, tossing well to evenly distribute the flavors. Allow the vegetables to soak in the marinade for approximately 25 minutes, mixing occasionally. The longer you allow them to soak, the more flavorful your end product will be.

3. While you are waiting for the vegetables to marinate, prepare the avocado sauce. Remove the skin and pits from the avocados. In a food processor, combine the avocados, cilantro, parsley, lime juice, and water. Blend until smooth and combined, adding salt and pepper to taste. Move the sauce to a small serving bowl.

4. In a large skillet, heat a tablespoon of olive oil over medium heat. When the oil is to temperature, add the previously marinated vegetables. Cook, stirring frequently, until all vegetables are cooked through and the peppers and mushrooms have begun to brown, approximately 8 or more minutes.

5. Gently warm the tortillas individually in a lightly oiled pan over medium-low heat, flipping halfway through cooking (about 20 seconds per tortilla). Place the tortillas in a tortilla warmer or an oven on low to keep warm. Add the cooked vegetable mix to each tortilla, topping with a dollop of avocado sauce and a sprinkle of cotija. Serve and enjoy!

Stuffed Portobello Mushrooms

Stuffed portobellos are a great way to make use of the large caps. The idea can be adapted in a number of different ways, filling the mushrooms with whatever you have on hand. For this recipe, we are going to implement a classic Italian trio: tomato, mozzarella, and fresh basil.

Ingredients:
Garlic butter

- 2 tablespoons butter
- 2 cloves garlic, crushed
- 1 tablespoon freshly chopped parsley

Mushrooms:

- 5-6 large Portobello Mushrooms
- 5-6 fresh mozzarella cheese balls
- 1 cup cherry tomatoes
- fresh basil

Balsamic Glaze:

- 1/3 cup balsamic vinegar
- 1 tablespoon brown sugar

Instructions:

1. Preheat the oven to high, usually indicated by a "broil" or "grill" setting. Move the oven rack to the middle of the oven.

2. To prepare the garlic butter, combine the butter, garlic, and parsley in a saucepan. Melt the mixture until the garlic becomes fragrant.

3. Remove the stems from the portobello mushrooms. Wash the caps thoroughly and dry well with a paper towel. Brush the smooth, non-gilled side of the mushrooms with the garlic butter. Place the mushrooms butter side down on a baking tray. Brush any leftover garlic butter on the insides of each cap.

4. Slice the mozzarella cheese balls into thin slices, approximately 1/4" thick. Slice the cherry tomatoes in a similar fashion, approximately 1/4" thick. Shred your fresh basil. Spread the tomato and mozzarella slices evenly around the caps. Bake the mushrooms in the oven until the cheese is melted and golden on top, approximately 7-10 minutes.

5. While the mushrooms are in the oven, you can prepare the balsamic glaze. Combine the brown sugar and vinegar in a saucepan over medium-high heat and bring to a boil. Once boiling, reduce heat to a low simmer for approximately 7 minutes, or until the mixture is thick and reduced to a glaze.

6. Remove the mushrooms from the oven. Apply a drizzle of balsamic glaze and a heavy sprinkle of basil to each mushroom. Serve and enjoy!

Mushroom Curry

Indian cuisine is known for its robust flavors, usually emphasized by spices like cardamom, cumin, and garam masala. This curry is no exception and employs a large array of spices that should not be too hard to find at most supermarkets or natural foods stores.

This mushroom curry is at its finest when paired with basmati rice or naan, a simple flatbread common in Indian cuisine and other parts of the world.

Ingredients:
Onion Paste
- 4 ounces of onions, about 1 cup when chopped
- 1 teaspoon chopped ginger
- 1 teaspoon chopped garlic

Tomato Puree
- 3 ounces of fresh tomato OR 1/2 cup canned tomato puree

Curry
- 8 ounces shiitake mushrooms
- 4 tablespoons plain Greek yogurt
- 3 tablespoon extra-virgin olive oil
- 1/2 teaspoon ground cumin
- 1 large bay leaf
- 1/4 teaspoon cinnamon
- 3 green cardamom seeds
- 3 cloves
- ¼ teaspoon ground turmeric powder
- ½ teaspoon red chili powder
- 1 teaspoon ground coriander powder
- ¼ teaspoon garam masala powder
- 2 tablespoon fresh cilantro leaves, chopped
- ¾ cup water or add as required
- salt to taste

Instructions:

1. Rinse the shiitake mushrooms thoroughly and dry completely with a paper towel. Slice or chop them to your liking and set them to the side.

2. To prepare the onion paste, start by roughly chopping your onions. Add the chopped onions, chopped ginger, and chopped garlic to a food processor or blender. Blend until it turns into a smooth paste (this should not require any water). Remove this paste with a spoon or spatula in a bowl. Keep this onion paste to the side.

3. To prepare the tomato puree, add the tomatoes (3 ounces or about 1/2 cup) to the same food processor or blender. Blend until the tomatoes are a smooth puree. Remove and set the tomato puree aside. If you are using canned tomato puree, this step can obviously be skipped.

4. Heat 3 tbsp extra virgin olive oil in a large pan and add the 1/2 tsp cumin seeds, 1/2 inch cinnamon, 3 green cardamom seeds, and 3 cloves. Sauté the spices until they become aromatic. Turn the heat on low and add the onion paste from step 2. Keep the pan on low and stir often. Continue to cook until the paste starts to thicken and eventually becomes a golden color. This process can take some time, so add a pinch of salt to speed it up if necessary.

5. Next, add the tomato puree. Stir and continue to cook on low for about 1 minute. Then add the ground spices: 1/4 tsp

113

turmeric powder, 1/2 tsp red chili powder and 1 tsp coriander powder. Continue cooking and stirring until oil begins to release from the sides of the mixture.

6. Add the chopped shiitake mushrooms and the yogurt. Stir well until the yogurt is completely combined. Simmer the curry on low for about 3 minutes. Add water as required to keep the mixture at a thick, soupy consistency. Add salt to taste and stir well. Cover the pan with a lid and simmer on low for about 15 minutes, or until the mushrooms are cooked through.

7. Remove the lid and add 1/4 tsp garam masala powder and 2 tbsp chopped cilantro leaves. Stir very well.

8. Serve and enjoy! This can be consumed by itself, similar to a thick soup, or it can be served with basmati rice or naan bread. The choice is yours!

Vegetarian "Beef" and Broccoli

Many recent studies have acknowledged the negative effect that red meat can have on someone's body. Frequent consumption of beef and other meat has been linked to an increased risk of cancer and other health problems. This vegetarian take on the classic Chinese take-out staple substitutes the beef for shiitake mushrooms!

Ingredients:

- 3 Tablespoons cornstarch
- 1 pound shiitake mushrooms
- 1/2 cup low sodium soy sauce
- 2 Tablespoons sesame oil, divided
- 4 cups small broccoli florets
- 1/2 cup white onions, sliced
- 3 Tablespoons packed light brown sugar
- 1 Tablespoon minced garlic
- 2 teaspoons grated fresh ginger
- White rice

Instructions:

1. Prepare enough white rice using your favorite method.

2. Rinse the shiitake mushrooms thoroughly and dry completely with a paper towel. Slice or chop them into 1/2 inch strips and set them to the side.

3. In a large bowl, whisk together 2 tablespoons of cornstarch with 3 tablespoons of water. Add the mushrooms to the bowl and toss to combine.

4. In a separate small bowl, whisk together the remaining 1 tablespoon cornstarch with the soy sauce, brown sugar, garlic and ginger. Set the sauce aside.

5. Heat a large nonstick frying pan over medium heat. Add 1 tablespoon of the sesame oil and once it is hot, add the mushrooms, stirring constantly. Cook for about 4-6 minutes, or until about halfway cooked through.

6. Add another tablespoon of sesame oil to the pan and add the broccoli florets and sliced onions. Cook, stirring or tossing occasionally, until the broccoli is tender, and the mushrooms are just about cooked through, or about 4 minutes.

7. Add the prepared sauce. Bring the mixture to a boil and cook, stirring, for 1 minute or until the sauce thickens slightly. Serve over white rice and enjoy.

Parmesan "Cheese"

Here is a great vegetarian/vegan alternative to parmesan cheese that harnesses the medicinal benefits of shiitake mushrooms. The cashews and walnuts combine to create a rich creamy feel, while the shiitake mushrooms and nutritional yeast provide the "umami" found in well-aged cheeses. Sprinkle it on any dish that calls for parmesan cheese to provide a boost of medicinal mushrooms.

Ingredients:

- 2 or 3 small, dried shiitake mushrooms
- ¼ cup nutritional yeast
- 1/2 teaspoon salt
- 2 ounces raw cashew nuts
- 1 ounce walnuts

Instructions:

1. Remove the ends of the stems from the dried shiitake mushrooms and add them to a food processor or blender. Add the nutritional yeast and salt. Blend until it turns into a powder and transfer the mixture to a bowl.

2. Add the walnuts to the food processor and pulse until it's crumbled but not too fine. Transfer this to the bowl from step 1.

3. Add the cashews to the food processor and pulse until crumbled but not too fine. Transfer to the bowl.

4. Stir the mixture together until it is uniform and well-combined.

5. Store in an airtight container in the refrigerator until use. Enjoy on any dish that calls for parmesan cheese!

Common Ailments

In this section, we will cover common ailments and the medicinal mushrooms that have been used to treat them. We will explore traditional remedies for the illnesses, as well as the current research that is being explored. You have seen some of this before as the species was described, where research had been completed. In those cases, the use was described to identify which mushroom would be most beneficial to improving health and primarily for fighting cancer.

Adaptogens

Adaptogenic substances are those that are claimed to stabilize physiological processes and promote homeostasis. The original definition of adaptogens involved any substance that may increase resistance to stress, but the meaning has evolved and morphed over time. Scientists and governing bodies do not currently have an agreement on what constitutes an adaptogen or their effectiveness, so labeling and advertising of "adaptogenic" products is currently frowned upon. However, recent research and studies have shed light on adaptogenic substances, and they seem to be found in a variety of medicinal mushrooms.

Depending on the definition, most medicinal mushrooms can be considered "adaptogens". Recently, the definition of adaptogen has expanded to mean a substance that performs a wide variety of functions, including "balancing bodily functions and enhancing wellness, vitality, strength, and vigor".

Grifola frondosa is often referred to as an adaptogen, as it has been shown to benefit many different aspects of the body. In traditional Chinese medicine, as well as other Asian countries nearby, *G. frondosa* has historically been used to treat a variety of health conditions, such as arthritis, hepatitis and HIV. Additionally, it was used to benefit the immune system.

In modern research, *G. frondosa* has been shown to have positive effects on cancerous tumors and the immune system. In lab studies on mice, the polysaccharides found in the fungus have been shown to have tumor-killing abilities. *G. frondosa* has been used in clinical human studies alongside conventional cancer treatments. The fungus helped relieve some of the negative effects of chemotherapy and radiation therapy. Another study with rodents was performed that showed the fungus' ability to aid in weight loss. Similar weight loss effects were recorded in human trials as well. Additionally, lab studies have shown that *G. frondosa* may help regulate blood glucose and cholesterol levels.

Ganoderma lucidum, one of the most popular medicinal mushrooms, is often considered to be an adaptogen due to its wide variety of benefits on the body. Research and traditional use have explored many positive effects of the fungus, such as antioxidant properties, enhanced immune response, slowing the spread of cancer, clearing respiratory issues, and aiding depression and fatigue.

The effects on cancer and co-treatment with modern medicine has been explored. In test tube environments, *G. lucidum* has been shown to kill cancer cells, including prostate cancer. The fungus has also been recorded as providing "better social well-being" to breast cancer survivors. One research publication found that the administration of *G. lucidum* alongside conventional cancer treatments can help improve the quality of life for patients, lessening some of the negative effects of chemotherapy and radiation therapy. Studies with groups of breast cancer survivors and neurasthenia patients have shown the fungus' effectiveness in reducing fatigue and depression. The results of animal lab studies and several human studies suggest that *G. lucidum* can help normalize blood glucose and cholesterol levels. Additionally, the triterpenes found in *G. lucidum* have been shown to lower blood pressure and prevent allergies.

Alzheimer's

Today, more than 5 million Americans are living with Alzheimer's disease, while worldwide Alzheimer's and dementia cases are estimated at 50 million. Alzheimer's patients often experience chronic inflammation and reduced blood flow in the brain, eventually leading to cell death and a loss of neuronal connections. Alzheimer's disease is the leading cause of dementia and is the 6th leading cause of death in the United States. There is no cure for Alzheimer's and most treatments only temporarily stop or slow the degenerative disease. For this reason, preventative care is essential and can be provided in part by medicinal mushrooms.

Auricularia auricula-judae has become a food of interest for the elderly, as it contains high levels of polysaccharides that have been shown to help defend against Alzheimer's disease. The anti-aging effects of *O. sinensis* have been explored. In a study involving older mice and rats, extracts from *O. sinensis* were shown to have improved the brain function and antioxidative activity in the rodents, as well as promoting sexual function. A similar study showed that extracts of *O. sinensis* can extend the lifespan of mice reverse many age-related changes in the mice.

Compounds found in some medicinal mushrooms, such as *Ganoderma lucidum*, and *Hericium erinaceus*, may have positive effects on brain health and could be considered for use in the treatment or management of depression, Alzheimer's, Huntington's, and Parkinson's diseases. Recently, a placebo-controlled trial was performed on Japanese men and women diagnosed with mild cognitive impairment. The patients were given 250 mg tablets containing *H. erinaceus* powder three times a day for 16 weeks. The results of the study concluded that *H. erinaceus* is effective in improving mild cognitive impairment.

Antibacterial

Antibacterial agents are intended to stop or slow the growth and spread of bacteria. Antibiotics are commonly used in modern medicine and can be highly effective. However, bacteria can become resistant to antibiotics when they are used too often, and antibiotic resistance has become a growing problem. Medicinal mushrooms have the possibility to aid this situation, as new forms of antibiotics are needed.

In a 2013 study, polysaccharides derived from *T. matsutake* were found to have strong antibacterial properties. The compound was used to fight off a range of bacteria, including *E. coli, Salmonella sp.*, and others. While it showed strong antimicrobial properties against all bacteria, it was found to be most effective against *Micrococcus lysodeikticus*.

The schizophyllan (SPG) found in *Schizophyllum commune* has also been explored for its possible protection against infections. SPG treated demonstrated protective effects against bacterial infections in mice, such as *P. aeruginosa, S. aureus, E. coli, and K. pneumoniae*. Similarly, SPG has been effective in protecting mice and Kuruma prawn against viral infections. The mice and shrimp had increased survival rates and higher virus-cell-killing activity when given oral doses of SPG. This leads one to infer that medicinal mushrooms are not only effective in mammals, but invertebrates like shrimp as well.

H. pylori is a common type of bacteria that grows in the digestive tract. Recently, a randomized trial of 25 patients compared the usefulness of *Hericium erinaceus* and essential oils against *H. pylori* infection. The study revealed that patients who received *H. erinaceus* tested negative for *H. pylori* in 89.5% of cases, while only 33.3% of patients tested negative after being treated with essential oils. The study concluded that *H. erinaceus* could be considered an alternative to antibiotic therapy against *H. pylori* and its associated diseases.

Anti-Inflammatory

Inflammation happens when your body's white blood cells (and the substances they create and secrete) protect you from infection, bacteria, viruses, or other foreign invaders. Chemicals from the white blood cells signal your body to raise blood flow to an injured or infected area, causing redness, warmth, and swelling. Inflammation can often go unseen as well, as in the case of heart, lung, or kidney inflammation. In some cases, such as with arthritis, the defense system doesn't know when to stop. Inflammation is triggered even when there are no outsiders to fight off. This is often the sign of an autoimmune disorder, in which the immune system overreacts and sometimes recognizes the regular, healthy components of your body as an enemy, causing excessive inflammation and damage. Chronic inflammation can last months or years and is often linked to a host of other conditions, including cancer, heart disease, asthma, Alzheimer's disease, and diabetes.

Medicinal mushrooms have long been identified as a source of relief for acute (short-lived) and chronic inflammation. Hippocrates, the Greek physician, was one of the first people to document and classify a mushroom. Around 450 BCE, he acknowledged the anti-inflammatory and wound-healing properties of *Fomes fomentarius*.

Auricularia auricula-judae contains high levels of polysaccharides that have anti-inflammatory activity. This builds off of *A. auricula's* traditional use for soothing irritated or inflamed mucous membranes.

When extract of the cultured mycelium of *Morchella esculenta* was administered to mice, the extract showed significant inhibition of both acute and chronic inflammation, comparable to the study's reference drug, Diclofenac.

Patients with ulcerative colitis, an inflammatory bowel disease, have seen improved quality of life when consuming *Agaricus blazei*.

In traditional Chinese medicine, *Geastrum triplex* has been used to reduce respiratory tract inflammation.

Extracts of *Trametes versicolor* contain krestin (PSK) and polysaccharide peptide (PSP). Both of these polysaccharides are known to promote immune response and suppress inflammation. One *in vitro* (test tube) study concluded that the PSP found in turkey tails can increase a type of white blood cell called monocytes.

These cells fight infection and inflammation, while also boosting immunity in the body.

One study with mice showed that extracts from *Inonotus obliquus* can reduce inflammation and damage in the gut by inhibiting inflammatory proteins.

Antioxidants

Antioxidants are substances that may prevent some types of cell damage. Antioxidants have the potential to prevent the negative effects of free radicals and oxidative stress. Free radicals can form in the body through natural ways including exercise and when your body converts food into energy. They can also enter the body from sources around you, such as air pollution, smoke, and sunlight.

Free radicals can cause oxidative stress, which is another term for cell damage. This phenomenon of oxidative stress has been suspected of contributing to a variety of diseases, including Alzheimer's disease, Parkinson's disease, cataracts, cancer, diabetes, and more. Therefore, antioxidants have been heavily researched and believed to aid in prevention of these diseases and other health problems. Free radicals may damage cellular lipids, proteins, and DNA, affecting their normal function and leading to various diseases.

Studies of a "polyphenolic extract" from the chaga mushroom (*Inonotus obliquus*) have indicated that the mushroom has strong antioxidant properties.

In a 2015 study, the antioxidative effects of *Taiwanofungus camphoratus* were explored. As the concentration of *T. camphoratus* was raised, the "radical-scavenging" effects of the fungus also increased. The results of the study suggested that *T. camphoratus* is a non-toxic antioxidant that could be added to health foods.

Cancer and Tumors

Cancer is one of the top causes of death worldwide. In 2018 alone, there were over 9 million cancer-related deaths. The International Agency for Research on Cancer suggests that by 2040, the number of cancer related deaths could increase to over 16 million per year. Cancer rates are higher in the more industrialized parts of the world. The rate of cancer occurrence usually increases as life expectancy and standard of living increase in a population.

Because of these harsh realities, the world deserves alternative forms of treatment for cancer, especially preventative care. Current treatments include chemotherapy, radiotherapy, hormone therapy, and surgery. These conventional treatments are not always effective and cause many harmful side effects in patients. Adding mushrooms to one's diet has been shown to offer both preventative and diagnostic care. Clearly, modern medicine has not figured out how to properly prevent and treat cancer, so all viable options should be considered. This is especially true for medicinal mushrooms, as the effects and benefits have been experimented with and documented for hundreds of years. Many medicinal mushrooms have successfully been used alongside modern medicine to lessen the negative effects of treatments such as chemotherapy and radiation therapy.

Lentinula edodes (shiitake) has been tested and shown to have anti-tumor properties in both animals and humans. This is due to a variety of chemicals present in the fungus, most notable of which is polysaccharide lentinan.

In some East Asian countries, *Trametes versicolor* (turkey tail) has been used alongside modern medicine to help fight cancer. A patient who undergoes surgery, chemotherapy, or radiation to treat cancer may also take extracts of turkey tail mushrooms due to their natural immune boosting properties. One publication reviewed 13 different studies that involved giving patients doses of turkey tail mushrooms alongside conventional cancer treatment. The study demonstrated that those with colorectal cancer, gastric cancer, or breast cancer had a 9% decrease in 5-year mortality rate compared to those who received chemotherapy alone. A similar review looked at 8 studies encompassing over 8,000 people who received PSK along with chemotherapy. The group that received PSK had a longer lifespan after surgery than the control group that received chemotherapy alone. Another study covered 11 women with breast cancer, some of which received a daily dose of turkey tail in powder form after each session of radiation therapy. The women who received the turkey tail showed an increase in the cancer fighting cells of the immune system, including natural killer cells and white blood cells.

Reishi mushrooms (*Ganoderma lucidum*) contain beta-glucans, a complex sugar that has been shown to stop the spread and growth of cancer cells in lab studies. *Auricularia auricula-judae* has also been found to contain glucans that exhibit strong anti-tumor properties when given to mice with sarcoma tumors. When extract of the cultured mycelium of *M. esculenta* was administered to mice with implanted tumors, the extracts also exhibited significant antitumor activity. A 2005 study helps confirm the antitumor results of the previously mentioned study. An extract of *M. esculenta* mycelium was orally administered to mice for 30 days, resulting in a 74% inhibition in tumor volume and a 79% decrease in tumor weight.

A 2013 study attempted to isolate the beneficial compounds found in *Tricholoma matsutake*. This study found that polysaccharides present in the fungus exhibit anti-tumor, immuno-stimulation, anti-oxidation, and other biological activities. When the isolated compound was given to lab mice with tumors, the tumors dramatically reduced in size compared to a control group. In addition, the appetite, activity, and fur of the mice increased in quality as they were given the mushroom-derived compound.

Similar studies have been performed with *Grifola frondosa* that reveal anti-tumor properties. Scientists in Japan have been working for the past few decades to isolate the polysaccharide found in maitake mushrooms, as it has been shown to have anti-tumor effects when used on lab animals. Clinical studies have also been performed with humans to judge the mushroom's effect on cancer-related issues. In a study featuring 165 patients, 90% of the people reported that their cancer-related issues, such as hair loss and nausea, had improved. In addition, 83% of the patients expressed a reduction in overall pain.

Studies have explored the effects of *A. blazei* and cancer treatment. Data from one study showed that a daily dose of *A. blazei* can improve cancer remissions patients' quality of life. Myeloma patients that have taken extracts of *A. blazei* have benefited from the immunomodulatory effects of the fungus. Normally, a range of pharmaceutical drugs are used as immunomodulators, but these drugs can have serious side effects. Thalidomide, lenalidomide, and pomalidomide are currently used for this purpose, and various side effects such as birth defects, skin irritation, and burning sensations have been recorded.

Fomes fomentarius has been studied for its effects on cancer. One such study successfully used extracts of the fungus to limit the growth of cancer cells in mice that were implanted with sarcoma, a form of cancer. Similarly, another study used *F. fomentarius* to successfully slow down and kill human breast cell cancers. This was done in a lab environment with "cultured cell lines", as opposed to a human clinical trial. In one study, laboratory mice were implanted with sarcoma, a form of cancer. Extracts from *F. fomentarius* were successfully used to limit the growth of cancer cells in the mice. In a similar study, the effects of *F. fomentarius* on human breast cancer cells was explored. In a test tube environment, *F. fomentarius* extracts successfully slowed and killed the breast cancer cells. Human clinical trials have not been widely performed.

The medicinal effects of *S. commune* have been studied extensively, mostly in lab studies involving animals. A beta-glucan, "schizophyllan" or "SPG", has been identified as a useful cancer treatment when combined with chemotherapy and radiation therapy. In mice implanted with tumors, SPG was shown to reduce the size of the tumors and extend survival time of the mice. The results were found by comparing the mushroom-treated mice with a control group of mice treated with only radiation. In similar studies, SPG was found to offer protective benefits to the bone marrow cells of mice that were receiving chemotherapy and radiation therapy. SPG was most effective against this radiation damage when given to the mice at the same time as radiation.

One report from Korea claims that after ingesting *P. linteus* for 18 months, a 65 year old man's hepatocellular carcinoma spontaneously regressed. Another report from Japan claimed that P. linteus had positive effects on a cancer patient with progressive bone metastasis. The most promising case study came from a 79 year old man who took a *P. linteus* extract for 1 month without any other treatment. After six months, his lung cancer completely regressed.

In test tube studies, extracts of *Cordyceps militaris* have been shown to have cytotoxic (cell-killing) effects on different types of cancer cells found in humans, including lung, skin, liver, and colon cancers. Additionally, a variety of species of *Cordyceps*, including C. militaris, have exhibited anti-tumor effects on mice implanted with lymphoma, melanoma, and lung cancer. Additionally, varieties of Cordyceps may be able to reverse the negative side effects associated with cancer therapies like radiation and chemotherapy. One side effect in particular, leukopenia, causes the number of white blood cells to decrease, slowing the body's natural defense system and increasing the risk of infection. In one study, mice were given radiation and chemotherapy drugs. Some mice developed leukopenia, which was then reversed by the administration of Cordyceps on said mice.

One study explored the effects of *Inonotus obliquus* in conjunction with traditional cancer treatments. They concluded that chaga is a strong immune modulator that can help the bone marrow system recover after being damaged by chemotherapy. The researchers also suggested that extracts of *I. obliquus* show potential for use as a supplement or therapeutic for people with compromised immune systems that have experienced bone marrow system damage. However, human clinical trials need to be performed to confirm these findings.

Other studies have looked at chaga's effects on tumors. One such in vitro (test tube) study demonstrated that extracts of *I. obliquus* could be used to inhibit the growth of tumors and kill existing cancerous cells. Another study was conducted that involved lab mice. Some mice were given extracts of *I. obliquus* for 3 weeks prior to being implanted with tumors. These mice experienced less tumor growth and a maintenance of body temperature. Additionally, the mice lost body weight. The researchers concluded that *I. obliquus* has the potential to be used as a natural cancer treatment and for general health care.

Another in vitro study demonstrated that extracts from *I. obliquus* have strong cytotoxic (cell-killing) against both mouse breast cancer cells and human breast cancer cells. They quote this as having to do with the triterpenes present in the fungus.

Diabetes

Diabetes refers to a group of diseases that result in too much sugar in the blood, also known as high blood glucose. According to the CDC, around 34 million Americans (over 10% of the population) have diabetes. Another 88 million people (over 33% of the population) has prediabetes, which is a set of symptoms that will eventually lead to diabetes if preventative care is not taken. Patients with Type 1 diabetes have a genetic disorder and cannot produce insulin, a substance in the body that helps process carbs, fats, and protein and regulates blood glucose levels. They almost always have to have daily injections of insulin. The necessary amount of insulin injections could possibly be lowered through the help of some of our medicinal mushrooms. More research is definitely warranted as diabetes affects such a large number of people.

In recent studies, diabetic mice were given a polysaccharide derived from wood ear mushrooms. The compound had a hypoglycemic effect on the mice and helped regulate their insulin, glucose, and food intake levels.

Several mushrooms, including *Auricularia auricula-judae, Ganoderma lucidum, Ganoderma frondosa, Hericium erinaceus,*

Inonotus obliquus, Ophiocordyceps sinensis, and others, are used in the production of functional foods for the prevention and treatment of diabetes.

Studies involving extracts of *Agaricus blazei* have shown the fungus' ability to improve insulin resistance in diabetic patients, while also reducing cholesterol, weight, and body fat in healthy people.

Experiments have indicated that *O. sinensis* has potential to aid diabetes in a variety of ways, including trigger the release of insulin, increase hepatic glucokinase, and increase sensitivity of cells to insulin. In a human clinical trial, 95% of diabetes patients treated with a daily dose of *O. sinensis* saw improvements in their blood sugar profile.

Fatigue and Physical Performance

Fatigue is a persistent feeling of tiredness. Most people experience fatigue intermittently, such as when you have the flu or when you didn't get enough sleep the night before. Chronic fatigue is often associated with other conditions, including depression, fibromyalgia, chronic kidney disease, lung disease, and more. Some people are simply diagnosed with "chronic fatigue", also known as systemic exertion intolerance disease. Fatigue can often be framed in the context of endurance: if someone has high endurance, then they don't fatigue easily. The opposite is true as well: if one has chronic fatigue, then they may not have prolonged endurance. Substances found in medicinal mushrooms have shown their potential as fatigue reducers and endurance boosters. These mushrooms have been used to benefit both high-achieving athletes and elderly people prone to fatigue.

Reishi mushrooms have also been shown to be effective against depression and fatigue. One study analyzed over 130 people with neurasthenia, a medical condition associated with emotional disturbance that causes fatigue, headaches, and irritability. The research found that the patients who were administered with *G. lucidum* had a greater sense of well-being and a decrease in fatigue. The researchers concluded that reishi mushroom had better results than a placebo in improving the symptoms associated with neurasthenia. A similar study covered a group of almost 50 breast cancer survivors. The women who received reishi mushroom powder over 4 weeks had reduced fatigue and improved quality of life versus a control group.

Recently, a study conducted on lab mice tested whether *O. sinensis* had an effect on endurance. After three weeks of consuming the fungus, the mice were able to swim significantly longer than the control groups that did not receive the supplement. The results were dependent on dose, as a lower dose inspired a 73% increase in endurance, while a higher dose only increased endurance by 30%. These studies confirm what traditional medicine has already known for centuries. In a similar study involving a group of twenty healthy elderly people, the subjects were either given doses of *O. sinensis* or a placebo. The group that received the fungus had improved measures of exercise performance, and the researchers suggested that *O. sinensis* "improves exercise performance and might contribute to wellness in healthy older subjects."

Gut Health

Gut health refers to the bacteria in the gastrointestinal tract and the way that they function and balance. In an ideal situation, the organs of the GI tract, such as the intestines, stomach, and esophagus, work in harmony to help us eat and digest food without any aches or pains. Unfortunately, approximately 60 to 70 million Americans are affected by digestive diseases, resulting in over 20 million hospitalizations and about 48 million ambulatory care visits in 2010. While some of the diseases associated with the gut are inherited or unavoidable, preventative care can go a long way in defending your gut from bacterial invaders and the like. Natural foods of all sorts can help promote good gut health and medicinal mushrooms are no exception.

H. pylori is a common type of bacteria that grows in the digestive tract, attacking the stomach lining and forming ulcers. It can be found in around 60% of the world's adult population. Recently, a randomized trial of 25 patients compared the usefulness of *H. erinaceus* and essential oils against *H. pylori* infection. The study revealed that patients who received *H. erinaceus* tested negative for *H. pylori* in 89.5% of cases, while only 33.3% of patients tested negative after being treated with essential oils. The study concluded that H. erinaceus could be considered an alternative to antibiotic therapy against *H. pylori* and its associated diseases.

T. versicolor also has the ability to enhance gut health. The mushrooms contain prebiotics, which helps promote good gut bacteria. One study compared the effects of turkey tail mushrooms and amoxicillin (an antibiotic) on gut health. The study lasted 8 weeks and involved 24 healthy patients, each of which was given either a polysaccharide extract from *T. versicolor*, amoxicillin, or a placebo. The patients that received amoxicillin had substantial changes to their gut biome that took weeks to recover. The patients that received *T. versicolor* had "clear and consistent microbiome changes consistent with its activity as a prebiotic."

Heart Health

According to the CDC, heart disease is the leading cause of death for men and women in the United States. One person dies every 36 seconds in the U.S. from cardiovascular disease. Diabetes, obesity, unhealthy diet, physical inactivity, and excessive alcohol consumption can all lead to a higher risk of heart disease and associated conditions. While addressing these conditions and lifestyle choices should be the first step towards preventative heart care, many medicinal mushrooms have also been used and tested to aid the heart and cardiovascular system. The underlying causes of heart disease (diabetes, obesity, etc.) may also benefit from the use of medicinal mushrooms, as made evident in different sections of this book.

The positive effects of *O. sinensis* on heart health has been widely researched. In China, *O. sinensis* has been used to treat arrhythmia, a condition related to irregular and slow heartbeats. In a study involving rats with chronic kidney disease, administration of

O. sinensis reduced injuries to the heart in these rats. Chronic kidney disease is known to cause heart injuries and can often lead to heart failure. The results of this study are promising, revealing the fungus as a possible preventative care for patients with chronic kidney disease.

Additionally, a variety of *Cordyceps* species have been shown to have beneficial effects on cholesterol levels. Higher cholesterol levels have often suggested poor heart health and an increased risk of heart disease. Research in rodents has suggested that Cordyceps may decrease LDL cholesterol, also known as the "bad" cholesterol. LDL raises the risk of heart disease, due to its tendency to cause a buildup of cholesterol in the arteries.

A recent human trial analyzed 26 people over a 12-week period. The patients who received *Ganoderma lucidum* had increased levels of HDL cholesterol (the "good" cholesterol). The patients also exhibited a lower level of triglycerides, a measure of certain fats in your blood.

Immune System

The overall purpose of the immune system is to prevent or limit infection. The lack of a properly functioning immune system is made clear by immune-compromised people, such as those with HIV, genetic immune disorders, or even pregnant women. These groups of people are susceptible to and often infected by bacteria and viruses that do not affect most healthy people. The immune system works by identifying dangerous, unhealthy cells and distinguishing them from healthy cells. These damaged cells may have been caused by infectious bacteria and viruses, or by other means, such as cancer or a wound. When a healthy immune system receives signals of an issue, it responds by sending the appropriate "workers" to fix the problem. If the immune system does not react in time or reacts improperly, then infections and further complications can occur. Similarly, an immune system can overreact or react without cause, leading to allergic reactions and other issues.

Many medicinal mushroom species have been researched and identified to have positive effects on the body's immune system. *Trametes versicolor*, also called Turkey tails, produce krestin and polysaccharide peptide (PSP), both of which are polysaccharides that contain strong immune-boosting properties. Studies done in test tubes have shown that PSP has the ability to increase white blood cell count to help fight infection and boost immunity.

In studies involving reishi mushrooms (*Ganoderma lucidum*) and lab animals, the immune systems of the lab animals became more active when introduced to the beta-glucans present in reishi mushrooms. Beta-glucans are a complex sugar that has been used to help stop the growth and spread of cancer cells in lab studies.

One study explored the immunomodulatory effects of *Inonotus obliquus*. They concluded that chaga is a strong immune modulator that can help the bone marrow system recover after being damaged by chemotherapy. The researchers also suggested that extracts of *I. obliquus* show potential for use as a supplement or therapeutic for people with compromised immune systems that have experienced bone marrow system damage.

The polysaccharides found in *Phellinus linteus* have been shown to have immune boosting properties. One study performed an experiment with mice that were implanted with melanoma cells. The mice that were treated with *P. linteus* survived significantly longer than control groups. One important note was that the compounds in *P. linteus* do not directly kill the cancer cells, but instead they stimulate the body's immune response to fight off the cancer itself.

In one study, polysaccharides derived from *Tremella fuciformis* were found to have a variety of benefits. These include stimulating the growth of immune organs such as the spleen and thymus, increasing the number and activities of many different cell types, and enhancing T-cell immune response.

Respiratory Problems

Respiratory disease is any type of disease that affects the lungs or other parts of the respiratory system. Respiratory diseases include asthma, pneumonia, lung cancer, pulmonary fibrosis, and chronic obstructive pulmonary disease (COPD). These diseases can be caused by infection, smoking, and air pollution. Other respiratory illnesses include coughing, bronchitis, and emphysema.

Medicinal mushrooms have been known to help treat and prevent many of these conditions. This is usually accomplished through the anti-inflammatory and anti-tumor (in the cases of cancer) properties found in the mushrooms.

In traditional Chinese medicine, earthstar mushrooms (*Geastrum triplex*) have been used to reduce respiratory tract inflammation. TCM also uses reishi mushrooms (*Ganoderma lucidum*) to stop respiratory issues such as coughing, wheezing, and phlegm. TCM has described uses for *Tremella fuciformis* in cough syrups and to treat respiratory illnesses. In addition, traditional Chinese medicine used species of *Morchella* to treat phlegm and breathing issues.

Traditional Chinese medicine says that *P. umbellatus* is a fungus that can drain "dampness". Dampness is thought of as too much moisture in the body, whether that be excessive water retention, phlegm, mucus, or other conditions.

Weight Loss

According to data from the CDC, the prevalence of obesity in America increased from 30.5% to 42.4% from 2000 to 2017, while the prevalence of severe obesity increased from 4.7% to 9.2%. These levels of obesity have led to related conditions being among the leading causes of death in the U.S., including heart disease, stroke, type 2 diabetes, and certain types of cancer. These diseases could mostly be avoided if preventative care was practiced and valued. Edible mushrooms provide a nutritious food source that is usually effective for weight loss, while some compounds found in medicinal mushrooms have been shown to increase the body's ability to lose weight.

Multiple studies have been made to determine the effects of *Grifola frondosa* on obesity. In a lab study, overweight rats were given a daily dose of maitake in powder form. These rats lost more weight than the control group over 18 weeks. In a similar observational study with humans, patients were given maitake tablets every day for two months. Thirty of the patients reported a loss in weight of up to 26 pounds. However, this was an uncontrolled study and should be taken with a grain of salt.

Mushrooms and mushroom-rich nutrition are regarded as healthy dietary food supplements to prevent and treat widespread weight problems, as well as diabetes. The results of animal lab studies and several human studies suggest that medicinal mushrooms *Ganoderma lucidum, Grifola frondosa, H. erinaceus, Phellinus linteus,* and different *Pleurotus* species can help normalize blood glucose and cholesterol levels.

Conclusion

With all of the information, studies, and testimonials available to us, it is hard to deny the abilities of medicinal mushrooms. While caution is understandable regarding mushrooms as a "cure" for any one thing, it is undeniable that the general public could benefit from increased consumption and exposure to natural remedies like medicinal mushrooms.

Much of the world, including America, relies heavily on the pharmaceutical industry. While modern medicine has certainly provided us with innumerable breakthroughs in human health, their "cures" often cause more problems than they solve. The opioid epidemic has been raging for decades, but doctors and the pharmaceutical industry continue to over-prescribe these drugs. While they may not admit it, it is safe to assume that profits play a big role in which drugs are prescribed, even when these drugs continually ruin people's lives. Natural alternatives to modern medicine deserve a closer look.

Nature did not provide us with mushrooms to turn a profit. When the correct species are foraged or cultivated in a positive manner, medicinal mushrooms are pure of heart and do not have many (or any) negative side-effects. If we look through the lens of traditional Chinese medicine, it is easy to see that we are missing a "holistic" approach to health in Western medicine. Preventative care does not hold the importance that it should, as a nutritious diet, exercise, and fresh air can solve and prevent many of the illnesses and diseases that are prevalent in modern society.

Hopefully this book has inspired you to do your own research, find new ways of living, and discover new ways to treat some of your ailments. Medicinal mushrooms are an untapped resource and we have only begun to scratch the surface of the many ways that they can benefit human lives.

Sources

Agrawal, D. C., & Dhanasekaran, M. (2019). *Medicinal mushrooms: Recent progress in research and development.* Springer.

American Cancer Society guideline for diet and physical activity for cancer prevention. (n.d.). American Cancer Society | Information and Resources about for Cancer: Breast, Colon, Lung, Prostate, Skin. https://www.cancer.org/healthy/eat-healthy-get-active/acs-guidelines-nutrition-physical-activity-cancer-prevention.html

Anticancer activity of subfractions containing pure compounds of Chaga mushroom (Inonotus obliquus) extract in human cancer cells and in Balbc/c mice bearing Sarcoma-180 cells. (n.d.). KoreaMed Synapse. https://synapse.koreamed.org/articles/1051060

Antigenotoxic effect of Trametes spp. Extracts against DNA damage on human peripheral white blood cells. (n.d.). PubMed Central (PMC). https://www.ncbi.nlm.nih.gov/pmc/articles/PMC4517545/

Anti-inflammatory activity of Pleurotus ostreatus, a culinary medicinal mushroom, in Wistar rats. (n.d.). PubMed Central (PMC). https://www.ncbi.nlm.nih.gov/pmc/articles/PMC7077046/

Anti-inflammatory and anti-nociceptive effects of the methanol extract of fomes fomentarius. (2004, October). PubMed. https://pubmed.ncbi.nlm.nih.gov/15467201/

Anti-inflammatory and Immunomodulating properties of fungal metabolites. (9). PubMed Central (PMC). https://www.ncbi.nlm.nih.gov/pmc/articles/PMC1160565/
Anti-microorganism, anti-tumor, and immune activities of a novel polysaccharide isolated from Tricholoma matsutake. (2013).

PubMed Central (PMC).
https://www.ncbi.nlm.nih.gov/pmc/articles/PMC3732428/

Antioxidant effect of Inonotus obliquus. (n.d.). ScienceDirect.com |
Science, health and medical journals, full text articles and books.
https://www.sciencedirect.com/science/article/abs/pii/S037887410
400457X

Antioxidants: In depth. (n.d.). NCCIH.
https://www.nccih.nih.gov/health/antioxidants-in-depth

Antioxidants of edible mushrooms. (n.d.). PubMed Central (PMC).
https://www.ncbi.nlm.nih.gov/pmc/articles/PMC6331815/

Antitumour, antimicrobial, antioxidant and
Antiacetylcholinesterase effect of Ganoderma Lucidum terpenoids
and polysaccharides: A review. (n.d.). PubMed Central (PMC).
https://www.ncbi.nlm.nih.gov/pmc/articles/PMC6017764/

Beneficial effects of edible and medicinal mushrooms on health
care. Ikekawa T - *Int J Med Mushr. 2001*;3(4):8-12.

Cancer Today. (n.d.). Global Cancer Observatory.
https://gco.iarc.fr/today/home

Chaga mushroom. (n.d.). Memorial Sloan Kettering Cancer
Center. https://www.mskcc.org/cancer-care/integrative-
medicine/herbs/chaga-mushroom

Chemical and medicobiological properties of chaga (review).
(n.d.). Pharmaceutical Chemistry Journal.
https://link.springer.com/article/10.1007/s11094-006-0194-4

Chuanxin Wang - OM Clinical / Faculty Supervisor. (n.d.). What is
the traditional Chinese medicine (TCM) model of the body?
Acupuncture and Massage College | Miami, FL | ACAOM
Accredited Acupuncture School.
https://www.amcollege.edu/blog/tcm-model-body-functional-
entities

Cloning and expression analysis of phenylalanine ammonia-lyase
gene in the mycelium and fruit body of the edible mushroom

Flammulina velutipes. (n.d.). PubMed Central (PMC). https://www.ncbi.nlm.nih.gov/pmc/articles/PMC4630440/

Continuous intake of the Chaga mushroom (Inonotus obliquus) aqueous extract suppresses cancer progression and maintains body temperature in mice. (n.d.). PubMed Central (PMC). https://www.ncbi.nlm.nih.gov/pmc/articles/PMC4946216/

Cordyceps as an herbal drug - Herbal medicine - NCBI bookshelf. (n.d.). National Center for Biotechnology Information. https://www.ncbi.nlm.nih.gov/books/NBK92758/

Cultivation of oyster mushrooms. (2016, June 27). Penn State Extension. https://extension.psu.edu/cultivation-of-oyster-mushrooms

Edible mushrooms: Improving human health and promoting quality life. (n.d.). PubMed Central (PMC). https://www.ncbi.nlm.nih.gov/pmc/articles/PMC4320875/

Effect of Cs-4® (Cordyceps sinensis) on exercise performance in healthy older subjects: A double-blind, placebo-controlled trial. (2010, May 18). Mary Ann Liebert, Inc., publishers. https://www.liebertpub.com/doi/abs/10.1089/acm.2009.0226

Effect of polysaccharide from Cordyceps militaris (Ascomycetes) on physical fatigue induced by forced swimming. (n.d.). PubMed. https://pubmed.ncbi.nlm.nih.gov/28094746/

Effect of shiitake (Lentinus edodes) and maitake (Grifola frondosa) mushrooms on blood pressure and plasma lipids of spontaneously hypertensive rats. (n.d.). PubMed. https://pubmed.ncbi.nlm.nih.gov/3443885/

Effects of amycenone on serum levels of tumor necrosis factor-α, interleukin-10, and depression-like behavior in mice after lipopolysaccharide administration. (n.d.). PubMed. https://pubmed.ncbi.nlm.nih.gov/26150007/

Effects of extracts of Coriolus versicolor (I'm-yunity) on cell-cycle progression and expression of interleukins-1 beta,-6, and -8 in promyelocytic HL-60 leukemic cells and mitogenically stimulated

and nonstimulated human lymphocytes. (n.d.). PubMed.
https://pubmed.ncbi.nlm.nih.gov/12470440/

Fermented beverages of pre- and Proto-historic China. (21,
December). PubMed Central (PMC).
https://www.ncbi.nlm.nih.gov/pmc/articles/PMC539767/

Final period. (n.d.). Encyclopedia Britannica.
https://www.britannica.com/science/traditional-Chinese-
medicine/Final-period

Fomes fomentarius (MushroomExpert.Com). (n.d.).
MushroomExpert.Com.
https://www.mushroomexpert.com/fomes_fomentarius.html

Fungal basics - bryophyte. (2007, May 4). Australian National
Botanic Gardens - Botanical Web Portal.
https://www.anbg.gov.au/bryophyte/case-studies/fungal-
basics.html

Fungi for the biological control of insect pests. (n.d.). eOrganic -
Science, experience and regulation based information on organic
farming and research. https://eorganic.org/node/2597

Ganoderma lucidum (Lingzhi or Reishi) - Herbal medicine - NCBI
bookshelf. (n.d.). National Center for Biotechnology Information.
https://www.ncbi.nlm.nih.gov/books/NBK92757/

The genus amanita (MushroomExpert.Com). (n.d.).
MushroomExpert.Com. Retrieved October 27, 2020, from
https://www.mushroomexpert.com/amanita.html

Identifying the "Mushroom of immortality": Assessing the
Ganoderma species composition in commercial Reishi products.
(n.d.). PubMed Central (PMC).
https://www.ncbi.nlm.nih.gov/pmc/articles/PMC6055023/

Immune modulation from five major mushrooms: Application to
integrative oncology. (n.d.). PubMed Central (PMC).
https://www.ncbi.nlm.nih.gov/pmc/articles/PMC4684115/

Immunomodulatory activity of the water extract from medicinal mushroom Inonotus obliquus. (n.d.). PubMed Central (PMC). https://www.ncbi.nlm.nih.gov/pmc/articles/PMC3774877/

Improving effects of the mushroom Yamabushitake (Hericium erinaceus) on mild cognitive impairment: A double-blind placebo-controlled clinical trial. (n.d.). PubMed. https://pubmed.ncbi.nlm.nih.gov/18844328/

Inonotus obliquus (MushroomExpert.Com). (n.d.). MushroomExpert.Com. https://www.mushroomexpert.com/inonotus_obliquus.html

Lindequist, U (2011) The impact of ethnomycology on modern pharmacy. *Curare 34*(1+2):118–123

Lentinula. (n.d.). Encyclopedia Britannica. https://www.britannica.com/science/Lentinula#ref1181939

Maitake. (n.d.). Drugs.com. https://www.drugs.com/npp/maitake.html

Maitake D-fraction, a natural mushroom extract, synergizes with interleukin-2 for increased lytic activity of peripheral blood mononuclear cells against various human tumor cell histologies. (2012, April 15). Cancer Research. https://cancerres.aacrjournals.org/content/72/8_Supplement/3515

Medicinal mushrooms: Towards a new horizon. (2010). PubMed Central (PMC). https://www.ncbi.nlm.nih.gov/pmc/articles/PMC3249912/

Medicinal mushrooms as an attractive new source of natural compounds for future cancer therapy. (26). PubMed Central (PMC). https://www.ncbi.nlm.nih.gov/pmc/articles/PMC6044372/

Medicinal mushrooms, *Taiwanofungus camphoratus*, spent culture broth, 3-isobutyl-1-methoxy-4-(4'-(3-methylbut-2-enyloxy)phenyl)-1*H*-pyrrole-2,5-dione, 5-(hydroxymethyl. (n.d.). Begell House Digital Library. https://www.dl.begellhouse.com

/journals/708ae68d64b17c52,52f67ca6221cc3fa,0978a9a87d143
39f.html

Medicinal value of the caterpillar fungi species of the genus
Cordyceps (Fr.) Link (Ascomycetes). A Review. Holliday J,
Cleaver M. *Int J Med Mushr, 2008;10*(3):219–234.

The mushroom Agaricus blazei Murill elicits medicinal effects on
tumor, infection, allergy, and inflammation through its modulation
of innate immunity and amelioration of Th1/Th2 imbalance and
inflammation. (n.d.). PubMed Central (PMC).
https://www.ncbi.nlm.nih.gov/pmc/articles/PMC3168293/

Mushroom | Definition, characteristics, species, & facts. (n.d.).
Encyclopedia Britannica.
https://www.britannica.com/science/mushroom

Mycelium. (n.d.). Encyclopedia Britannica.
https://www.britannica.com/science/mycelium

National Diabetes statistics report, 2020. (2020, August 9).
Centers for Disease Control and Prevention.
https://www.cdc.gov/diabetes/data/statistics-report/index.html

NCI Dictionary of cancer terms. (n.d.). National Cancer Institute.
https://www.cancer.gov/publications/dictionaries/cancer-
terms/def/respiratory-disease

Neural plasticity in the ageing brain. (n.d.). PubMed.
https://pubmed.ncbi.nlm.nih.gov/16371948/

Neurohealth properties of Hericium erinaceus mycelia enriched
with Erinacines. (n.d.). PubMed Central (PMC).
https://www.ncbi.nlm.nih.gov/pmc/articles/PMC5987239/

New North American standards for TCM medicinal mushroom.
(n.d.). ITC. https://www.intracen.org/itc/blogs/market-insder/New-
North-American-Standards-for-TCM-Medicinal-Mushroom/

Novel medicinal mushroom blend as a promising supplement in
integrative oncology: A multi-tiered study using 4T1 triple-negative

mouse breast cancer model. (n.d.). PubMed Central (PMC). https://www.ncbi.nlm.nih.gov/pmc/articles/PMC7279026/

Obesity is a common, serious, and costly disease. (2020, June 29). Centers for Disease Control and Prevention. https://www.cdc.gov/obesity/data/adult.html

Oral administration of soluble β-glucans extracted from Grifola frondosa induces systemic antitumor immune response and decreases immunosuppression in tumor-bearing mice. (n.d.). PubMed. https://pubmed.ncbi.nlm.nih.gov/23280601/

Philip G. Miles, Shu-Ting Chang - Mushrooms: Cultivation, Nutritional Value, Medicinal Effect, and Environmental Impact (2004, CRC Press)

Pleurotus ostreatus - the oyster mushroom, Hiratake, Ping gu, 平

菇. (n.d.). MedicalMushrooms.net.

https://www.medicalmushrooms.net/pleurotus-ostreatus-oyster-

mushroom/

Polysaccharides in fungi. XIV. Anti-inflammatory effect of the polysaccharides from the fruit bodies of several fungi. Ukai S, Kiho T, Hara C, Kuruma I, Tanaka Y. *J Pharmacobiodyn. 1983;6*(12):983-90.

Positive health online | Issue - 139. (n.d.). Positive Health Onlinepage - Welcome to PositiveHealthOnline USA. https://www.positivehealth.com/issue/issue-139-september-2007

Preclinical and clinical studies of Coriolus versicolor polysaccharopeptide as an immunotherapeutic in China. (n.d.). PubMed. https://pubmed.ncbi.nlm.nih.gov/28595034/

PSP activates monocytes in resting human peripheral blood mononuclear cells: immunomodulatory implications for cancer treatment. (n.d.). PubMed. https://pubmed.ncbi.nlm.nih.gov/23497877/

Purification and partial characterization of a novel hemagglutinating glycoprotein from the cultured mycelia of Hericium erinaceus. (n.d.). ScienceDirect.com https://sciencedirect.com/science/article/pii/S1359511314002323

Recent progress of research on medicinal mushrooms, foods, and other herbal products used in traditional Chinese medicine. (2012, April). PubMed Central (PMC). https://www.ncbi.nlm.nih.gov/pmc/articles/PMC3942920/

Reishi mushroom. (n.d.). Memorial Sloan Kettering Cancer Center. https://www.mskcc.org/cancer-care/integrative-medicine/herbs/reishi-mushroom

Rhodiola crenulata- and Cordyceps sinensis-based supplement boosts aerobic exercise performance after short-term high-altitude training. (1, September). PubMed Central (PMC). https://www.ncbi.nlm.nih.gov/pmc/articles/PMC4174424/

Spore | Definition, types, & examples. (n.d.). Encyclopedia Britannica. https://www.britannica.com/science/spore-biology

The effects of dietary supplementation with Agaricales mushrooms and other medicinal fungi on breast cancer: Evidence-based medicine. (n.d.). PubMed Central (PMC). https://www.ncbi.nlm.nih.gov/pmc/articles/PMC3226611/

The immunomodulatory potential of natural compounds in tumor-bearing mice and humans. (n.d.). PubMed Central (PMC). https://www.ncbi.nlm.nih.gov/pmc/articles/PMC6508979/

The pharmacological potential of mushrooms. (n.d.). PubMed Central (PMC). https://www.ncbi.nlm.nih.gov/pmc/articles/PMC1193547/

The TCM channel system (Jing Luo). (n.d.). Taking Charge of Your Health & Wellbeing. https://www.takingcharge.csh.umn.edu/explore-healing-practices/what-traditional-chinese-medicine/what-qi-and-other-concepts/-tcm-channel-

Traditional uses and medicinal potential of Cordyceps sinensis of Sikkim. (2011, January). PubMed Central (PMC). https://www.ncbi.nlm.nih.gov/pmc/articles/PMC3121254/

Trametes versicolor: The Turkey tail (MushroomExpert.Com). (n.d.). MushroomExpert.Com. https://www.mushroomexpert.com/trametes_versicolor.html

Trametes versicolor mushroom immune therapy in breast cancer. (n.d.). PubMed Central (PMC). https://www.ncbi.nlm.nih.gov/pmc/articles/PMC2845472/

Turkey tail fungus. (n.d.). Macalester College. https://www.macalester.edu/ordway/biodiversity/inventory/turkeytailfungus/

Utah State University. (n.d.). Collect and identify. Intermountain Herbarium - USU. https://herbarium.usu.edu/fun-with-fungi/collect-and-identify

Utah State University. (n.d.). Earth stars | Herbarium. Intermountain Herbarium - USU. https://herbarium.usu.edu/fun-with-fungi/earth-stars

Winkler, D. (2009). "Caterpillar Fungus (Ophiocordyceps sinensis) Production and Sustainability on the Tibetan Plateau and in the Himalayas" (PDF). Asian Medicine. 5 (2): 291–316

Ying J-Z, Xiao-Lan M (1987). Icones of Medicinal Fungi in China. Beijing, China: Science Press. pp. 527–28. ISBN 978-7-03-000195-5.

www.ingramcontent.com/pod-product-compliance
Lightning Source LLC
Chambersburg PA
CBHW070117030426
42335CB00016B/2187